BECOMING THE
REAL YOU

SELECTED NUGGETS OF WISDOM FOR PERSONAL AND SPIRITUAL GROWTH

PHIL CAWLEY

CONTENTS

Preface

Introduction

Chapter 1 The Mind – The Most Powerful Tool We Possess

Chapter 2 I Think Therefore I Am *Descartes*

Chapter 3 Words of Wonder or Words That Wound

Chapter 4 Prosperity Within

Chapter 5 I am Grateful

Chapter 6 Humble Pie

Chapter 7 Forgive to live

Chapter 8 Affirmation Ignites Creation

Chapter 9 Visualise to Materialise

Chapter 10 Fear Not

Chapter 11 The Secret Place

Chapter 12 Journaling – Write Your Day

Chapter 13 Healthy Body, Healthy Mind *"food for thought"*

Chapter 14 Power Hour, Mighty Morning

Conclusion

Preface

This book is a reflection of several years of study into living the pre-determined life we are all designed to live.

We are all blessed with a unique blue print, a road map or GPS to take us from small and humble beginnings to running our race and finishing well, but most of us get a bit side tracked on the way.

Typically, we have dreams as a child where nothing is impossible, "child-like faith", we are invincible, powerful, full of imagination, creativity and adventure.

We all remember the wonder years, waking up early morning in the holiday period to a huge wealth of opportunity held in a new day, having dragged ourselves, reluctantly, out of bed all school term, we now have an in-built alarm clock, renewed vigour and drive. Pull on t-shirt, jeans and sneakers in record breaking time, and inhale breakfast in eager anticipation of the excitement of another long summer's day. This was my memory of childhood, so much colour, passion and elation and this was usually ignited by a planned fishing trip or bike ride, nothing special you may think, but it was special, every day was special, the friendships, the countryside, the scents, the sounds, the feeling of being alive.

Why does this lust for life have to die as we get older? It doesn't, or at least it shouldn't, and in this book, I hope to shed some light on recapturing the quintessential essence, contentment and peace of being who we are really meant to be.

Then God said "let us make man in Our image, according to Our likeness" (Genesis 1:26) ....Then later in the New Testament Jesus says "Therefore you are to be perfect, as your heavenly Father is perfect" (Mathew 5:48).

Introduction

Two profound statements from both the old and new testaments of the Bible which are equally mind-blowing, giving credit to human beings as having divine qualities and capabilities, and challenging us to strive for perfection in the eyes of a creator. We will never attain true perfection in this life as pointed out in the book of Romans "none are righteous, no, not one" (Romans 3:10), but we are challenged to strive to be the best versions of ourselves in all facets of our lives. Whether you are of a Christian persuasion as I am, or you subscribe to another of the many world religions, cultures or groups, the fact remains that most of us would like to be the best we can in all the important areas of our lives, and to make a difference for the better to the world we live in, and to those around us.

It is all too easy for us to become stuck in our ways, accepting our perceived lot and wading about in our self-engineered mediocrity, but to make significant and positive life improvement we must have a paradigm shift. We are imprisoned by our own perception of reality and need to break through these perceived limitations by controlling how we look at things. However, "If you change the way you look at things, the things you look at change". We all fall victim to habits which govern the way we live our lives, whether good habits or bad, they seem to be in control. As Aristotle once said "we are what we repeatedly do. Excellence, then, is not an act but a habit".

Instead of being victims of circumstance, we can change our mindset by thinking in a different way, we can create our own reality, to be prosperous, happy and healthy, the limitations of the past do not have to shape our future. We can break free of the environmental shackles and perceived limitations of our external world, all the things we cling on to within our comfort zone which somehow justify and validate our current position in life with all its frustrations and disappointments. We can forge a new direction to travel, step away from what we are used to and begin to live, in our minds, the life we desire until it begins to become our reality.

Without vision we are effectively being shaped by past experience and our environment, both of which we are very familiar with and both of which have very predictable outcomes. By changing our thought patterns, we begin to rewire our brains creating new neuro pathways, we break out from the boundaries of the past. When we begin to think bigger than our past experience, we step out of the comfort zone into the quantum field where nothing is impossible, we begin to live from a position of expectation, eager anticipation and a new excitement. Once we begin to achieve this state of consciousness, we need to guard against falling back into old habits and norms that have only served to enslave and ensnare, and to press forward into new territory where dreams and destiny exist.

To make the shift into this enlightened and fresh way of thinking we need to be become disciplined and determined. Get into your "secret place", wherever that is, first thing in the morning, close the door on the world and all its distractions. An early morning 'power hour' is a practice I subscribe to as we are naturally more perceptive and in tune with our spirituality in the earlier hours. Sit quietly and tap into the divine nature of God, infinite intelligence, peace and tranquillity, and as you meditate on this, let go and get beyond yourself, your body, your circumstances, get beyond time and human sensation until all that is left is gratitude for this experience and thankfulness for this supernatural moment where divine power is readily available. This is a magical time where inspiration and creativity flow freely and can be impressed into the sub-conscious mind. When you begin to flow in these moments and pray and affirm with gratitude and passion your desires and dreams, you begin the process of bringing them into reality.

Be thankful and deeply grateful for all you have and all you are; for breath in your lungs and sight in your eyes, for strength and energy, faith and love, for family and friends, for a new day, for the sunrise, for divine inspiration, health and well-being, for material possessions, income and prosperity. Count your blessings every day.

Your thoughts, which become your words, will turn into your actions and lifestyle and will determine your level of success. Your health, and your happiness, your spiritual connectedness, temperament and longevity are dependent on this and it is crucial that we get it right. We must break bad habits of the past and move into a healthy mindset if we wish to achieve and be the best versions of ourselves.

See every challenge as a new opportunity, another thing you rise to and solve, making you a better person and more fulfilled than you were before the problem existed. Do not avoid perceived problems and so procrastinate doing what you know you need to do in order to achieve your goals. Thomas Edison, when seeking a way to invent the light bulb dismissed any short comings as a learning curve, he stated, "I have not failed, I've just found 10,000 ways that won't work", he then ultimately succeeded and changed the world.

The only way to get the benefit from this process and begin to become the person you really want to be is to get started, now is the time for change, jump in at the deep end then don't give up, change will come for the better if you stay with these principles. Always ensure your vision is bigger than your environment and circumstances, and don't be defined by your past. Your history does not have to be your future.

"Some men see things as they are, and say why? I dream of the things that never were, and say why not?" (George Bernard Shaw).

1 The mind – the most powerful tool we possess

"The mind is everything, what you think you become" Buddha.

The mind can take us into the depths of failure, or, to the optimal heights of success. We need to be fluent in the language of the mind and have a firm grasp on what we allow to take up residence there. Become the master of your mind or it will rule you, what you think about, you will attract. "What we think about when we are free to think about what we will – that is what we are, or will soon become" (A.W. Tozer). Whatever you hold in your mind will tend to occur in your life, positive thoughts will change your life for the better and negative thoughts will likewise attract the opposite. There is no limit to the power of the human mind and imagination, aside from the limitations we inflict on ourselves.

In this first chapter I hope to give a simplified description of the dynamics of the two main facets of the mind, and how a person can control their thoughts, feelings and behaviour. This area, as saturated as it is in terms of research, is still in its infancy and I apologise in advance, if, despite my efforts, it still seems a bit technical, but I assure you I am simplifying research as best I am able.

Autosuggestion and the sub-conscious mind:

To use a simple definition, the mind has two parts to it, the conscious mind and the sub-conscious mind. The conscious mind is the thinking side of the mind which is the highest function human beings are capable of; this is our educated mind, and we can think whatever we wish. In our conscious mind we have choice, we can choose to accept or reject anything. The sub-conscious mind however is not so guarded, it acts first on our dominant desires when they have been mixed with our emotions, these desires could be good or bad, positive or negative.

The conscious mind accounts for about 12% of the mind, and is the goal setter in the here and now, but it has no long-term memory. The sub-conscious mind on the other hand accounts for around 88% of the mind, it is the goal getter, it handles all human functions and it is programmable, it never forgets. We may have watched a film, or had a difficult conversation before retiring to bed, and the sub-conscious mind will continue to work with this information, working day and night, drawing on universal powers to find the physical equivalent to the information received. We can leave the doors of our sub-conscious mind wide open without realising, and ultimately absorb all kinds of material, good, or bad, from watching mindless TV shows or being privy to conversations we are not really paying attention to, or from gossip we hear in the work place. This is why when we are watching a TV show, or a film, our emotions can easily get involved with the on-screen experience, and we can feel angry or sad or happy, despite the drama being fictional, as our sub-conscious mind cannot tell the difference between real and imaginary.

The sub-conscious mind, conversely, is known as the link, or connection point between the finite and the infinite, where thoughts are changed to their spiritual equivalent, prayers and answers to prayers go through the sub-conscious mind. The sub-conscious mind is always active, so if we do not put things there on purpose, it will use thoughts which are there by default, due to our negligence. The sub-conscious mind also takes deposits which have first passed through the conscious mind but, conversely, it has no power to reject these thoughts, it is also the part of the mind where our emotions are held. The sub-conscious mind does not have the power to reject information, so it must accept everything, it cannot differentiate between what is real and what is imaginary, so this renders the sub-conscious mind to be extremely impressionable. Bob Proctor, (author and motivational speaker), in one of his online seminars explains this idea by using the analogy of the way hypnotists work; the subject is setting aside their conscious mind so that the sub-conscious mind will accept whatever they are told, so if they are given some embarrassing act to perform, they will carry it out obliviously.

Our blueprint on life, or our paradigm, is determined from a very early age. A paradigm is a thought pattern, or sub-conscious conditioning, which defines a person's basic assumptions and approach to something. Our sub-conscious mind is left wide open from birth, as babies cannot use their conscious minds, so only their sub-conscious minds are in play, and they are receiving information from all around. The baby therefore learns really quickly, their minds reject nothing, so language, and all areas of early development, come very swiftly to a child. This process continues throughout life, as more and more information is dumped into the sub-conscious, colouring the views of the person, information is being gathered from many areas including parents, peers, family, media etc. This early imprinting has a lasting effect on the individual, and if this information is of a negative flavour, offering a poor outlook on life, or doesn't see success and prosperity as important, or worse, has disdain or dislike for those successful in life, then this will become the blueprint of the individual and will likely be carried through to adulthood and beyond. A person's beliefs, political bent and self-image are all influenced in the same way and unless the person begins to think on purpose, with a desire to change their paradigm, they will probably follow in the footsteps of those who influenced them, and so, their success, and earning capacity will be roughly equated to those people around them. Bob Proctor argues that a person can have superior knowledge but get inferior results because they never changed their paradigm; hard work, study and knowledge has therefore been limited automatically by the blueprint in the sub-conscious mind.

Auto-suggestion as a concept was first introduced at the beginning of the 20th century by Emile Coue, and has then been developed over many years as a psychological technique closely related to the placebo effect. It is a self-induced suggestion, in which individuals can guide and control their thoughts, feelings and behaviour. His methods mainly focussed on dominant thought repetition, both at the beginning, and end of each day. Coue maintained that he was not a healer but that he was an enabler, helping people to heal themselves through sub-conscious thought and imagination. Coue made claims that organic changes can be made through auto-suggestion. This idea is now common knowledge within the realms of neuroscience and quantum physics. Coue's driving belief was that any idea, exclusively occupying the mind, turns into reality, either positive or negative.

Auto-suggestion, is suggestion to one's self, it is a communication between the conscious and the sub-conscious mind. Using dominant thoughts, either good or bad repeatedly, within the conscious mind, will ultimately influence the sub-conscious mind. All thoughts come first to the conscious mind, and a vetting of these thoughts takes place. If a person then chooses to, they can repeatedly pass, and affirm this information to the sub-conscious mind, and the sub-conscious mind will act on this information, as long as there is an investment of faith and the person engages their emotions. Success in auto-suggestion will only come through persistence, and it is an exact science, so it will work for all, but determination is the key. In the words of Napoleon Hill "Your ability to use the principal of auto-suggestion will depend, very largely, upon your capacity to concentrate upon a given desire until that desire becomes a burning obsession....the sub-conscious mind takes any orders given to it in a spirit of absolute faith, and acts upon those orders, although, the orders have to be presented over and over again, through repetition, before they are interpreted by the sub-conscious mind". Any thoughts when mixed with emotion will cause vibration, and will attract a like vibration due to magnetic force. From the infinite abundance of the universe, our minds are constantly attracting the vibrations which are in harmony with our own dominant thoughts, and, through audible repeated repetition these vibrations reach our subconscious mind. Whether we fill our subconscious minds with faith or fear, it will translate it into its physical equivalent, so we need to guard our thoughts and shape them through auto-suggestion to our desired end, "take every thought captive". On average we are only operating from our conscious mind for around 5% of the day, the rest of our thought is pre-programmed and repetitive, largely based on past experience, and it doesn't change easily, positive repetition is crucial to re-programme our sub-conscious mind.

Auto-suggestion is the mechanism by which we promote our wants and desires to our sub-conscious mind, by regular repetition and affirmation of our dominant thought process, we can create new habits. If we combine these repetitions of words, with faith, and a full investment of emotion, we have a combination that is essential to developing the sub-conscious mind. The method being explained here will work for everyone if followed correctly with determination and persistence.

2   I think therefore I am: *Descartes*

Our thoughts are crucial to how our lives begin to unfold and the vibrations we emanate, both positive and negative, are birthed in our thought processes. Many people have heard the famous quote by Henry Ford "whether you think you can or whether you think you can't, you're right". These are very intuitive words, and he clearly was not the first person to make such inferences about the significance of the mind. The Bible holds many verses about the power and importance of our thought processes. "As a man thinketh in his heart, so is he" (Proverbs 23:7). We are told that we have been given a spirit of power, love and a sound mind (2 Timothy 1:7). We are told to think on things that are right and pure and admirable and of good report (Philippians 4:8), and to be transformed by the renewing of our mind

(Romans 12:2). The importance of our thinking is emphasised again in scripture, when we are told to take every thought captive and make it obedient (2 Corinthians 10:5).

Our thought processes then are hugely important and are the foundation of everything in our material world. We think, we speak and we act, and there is nothing in the physical world that didn't start out as someone's thought. Andrew Carnigie, one of the most affluent and influential men of his time, quoted "any idea that is held in the mind, that is emphasised, and either feared or revered, will begin to cloth itself in the most convenient and appropriate form available". So, whatever you hold in your mind will tend to eventually occur in your life, if you continue to believe as you always have you will continue to act in the same way and get what you have always got. You cannot expect different results tomorrow whilst doing the same things you always do.

We can actually change the organic structure of our brain by the thoughts we think, a process known in quantum physics and associated sciences as neuroplasticity. This is the ability of the mind, which is the brain in action, through thought, to develop and grow new neurons and continually improve the mind, this is contrary to previous thought, that mind and brain capacity diminish with age.

We have, as a minimum 3 million years of space within the brain according to scientific research and we still only know about 10% of what the brain is capable of. The brain processes around 400 billion bits of information per second and yet we are only aware of around 2000 of these which pertain to our bodies and feelings. There is an endless scope of possibility in terms of our mental capacity, **we can break bad habits**. A habit is when the body becomes the mind, it is one and the same thing. Dr Caroline Leaf (Neuroscientist) suggests that we can create new habits by rewiring our neuro-pathways using similar methods of training the mind, she suggests 21 days of repetition to establish new pathways followed by another 2 sets of 21 days to establish a new habit. "The greatest discovery of any generation is that a human being can alter his life by altering his attitude" (William James).

By observing ourselves and how we think and feel we can reinvent ourselves, according to current thought, through the process of "mental rehearsal". Neuropsychologist Donald Hebb first used the phrase "neurons that fire together, wire together", this was in 1949 and it was used to explain how pathways in the brain are formed and reinforced by repetition. To create a path on earth we must walk over the ground repeatedly, and this is the same with the mind, to make a deep mental path we must think our desired thoughts over and over in order for them to become dominant in the mind. The realm of our thought is often referred to as the "quantum field" and our capacity in this area is limitless. The power of thought is such that we can boost our immune system by thinking differently, meditation can keep a person significantly younger. Our thoughts are energy and we can think deliberately and positively and enhance our lives, or, we can waste energy with toxic thoughts which ultimately brings negativity and disease. "The greatest weapon against stress is our ability to choose one thought over another" (William James-Psychologist).

I will mention Dr Joe Dispenza several times in this book and with good reason, as a leader in the field of neuroscience, lecturer and author he is an inspiration to many in the area of mind, thought and brain interaction. I have captured a brief summary of part of a lecture he calls "soul sessions".

Mind is the brain in action, we have 100 billion neurones that work together perfectly to produce millions of different actions. The brain is just another organ, so what changes and develops the mind is the consciousness. If we keep on living the same way with the same thoughts, emotions and habits (our personality) then we stay the same, if we begin thinking in new ways and break away from these traditions and habits, we begin to form new neuro pathways in the brain (neuroplasticity), forming new habits, emotions and experiences. As long as your thoughts are equal to your environment you will remain the same and keep producing the same experience and outcome. In order to change we need to begin to think greater than our environment. Feelings and emotions cause us to remember experiences more clearly, so if we view the future based on the feelings of past experience then we are living from the past, which makes change very difficult to achieve. We need to let go of the emotions of the past in order to move on. When we are angry or frustrated and over producing adrenalin, we tend to be reactionary and often do or say things we may later regret as we are swamped with surplus chemicals, creating for us a situation which is not reality. When we are acting and speaking intuitively, on the other hand, we are more in touch with our soul (mind, will and emotions) and we will tend to respond, not react, as we are in tune with our feelings. The first condition is living is survival, the latter is living in creation. Human beings can turn on stress by thought alone, bringing past emotions into present and perceived future events, our body's chemical reaction then knocks us out of balance our mind and body is incongruent. Our emotions and reactions become very self-centred and we become preoccupied with our perception of our environment. Conversely, when we are in a truly creative state, we become unaware of time and self and we become lost in the wonder of the moment where all things are possible. In this creative state the only thing that is real is our thoughts and the brain begins to see the thought as the experience and proceeds to upload the corresponding neurological hardware ahead of the event and we begin living in the present from the heart (Joe Dispenza).

We are a mass of energy moving at a very high rate of vibration, we are made up of fifty trillion cells which are all living entities controlled and governed by the mind. According to Albert Einstein "everything is energy and that's all there is to it, match the frequency of the reality you want, and you cannot help but get that reality, it can be no other way. This is not philosophy this is physics". "The moment your beliefs match with any state, you fuse with it, and this union results in the activation of, and projection of its plots, plans conditions and circumstances. This new state of conscious awareness becomes your home from which you view the world" (Bob Proctor).

We must control the flow of thought energy, letting it flow to us and through us to improve everything with which it connects, then if we are observant, we will see outer reality shaping itself to our imagination. We are limited only by our imagination. According to Socrates there is an invisible energy which he refers to as a "form" or "soul" and this energy has always been here, it is perfect and unchanging, the material world he sees as a corrupt shadow of this. Consciousness is the most fundamental part of life, consciousness is physics, we are connected to ultimate consciousness or ultimate intelligence, the divine source. Consciousness is awareness and awareness, is paying attention, so if we pay attention to our thoughts, we ought to be able to rewire our consciousness. We are triune beings, spirit, soul (mind, will and emotions) and body and the three parts work in synergy, the spirit controls the mind and the mind (brain in action) controls the body. The brain is the complex flesh part, the mind is you, and mind is over matter. As we think, feel and choose we make a genetic expression and chemicals move towards physical expression causing proteins to form into structures, tree-like in appearance. We are designed to be constantly developing, but we must choose this, if we are not growing, we are dying. According to Dr Joe Dispenza's extensive research in this field, there is an intelligence from within that we are connected to, when we disconnect from this intelligence, we get sick. Emotional mis-management of energy and attention cause stress and ultimately illness, the hormones produced here, get to be addictive, and we ultimately pursue a life we don't want, we need to break the habit of being ourselves. Dr Dispenza goes on to say that thoughts are electric and feelings are magnetic, we need to get bigger than our emotions to make a positive change. He suggests that we need to separate ourselves from our environment, focussed meditation can be key here, any changes we make can be significant real change. We should "aim to emulate the divine, the creator, let's not be seduced by the external environment and fall from grace". We get used to what is familiar in life, if you struggle to get out of bed in the morning, think back to what used to excite you about getting up when you were a young child.

Neuroscience states that we have a finite set of neural circuits and by the time we reach the age of 35 we stop learning. We "know enough" to achieve what we have come to expect from life now, doing our job well, raising a family etc, so nothing changes anymore we are mainly living from our feelings, it becomes harder and harder to change and new knowledge is essential here. Our perceived reality comes from our experiences and how we feel, and if we cannot think bigger than our feelings says Dr Joe Dispenza then nothing changes. If this process continues it becomes a temperament or a state of being, by 35 years old this has become our perceived identity. When we decide to change, new cells will begin to develop, new chemicals are now present which are contrary to our experience and we may choose to postpone the idea of change until another day as it is not a familiar experience. This is what the Apostle Paul was referring to in the book of Corinthians "Therefore I do not run like someone running aimlessly, I do not fight like a boxer beating the air, no I discipline my body like an athlete so that after I have preached to others I am not disqualified from the prize". (1 Corinthians 9:26-27). Paul is striving to follow the higher cause and is determined not to let any physical or emotional discomfort get in the way of his dominant desire. He speaks also in the book of Romans about pursuing higher knowledge and divine purpose when he said "be not conformed to this world; but be transformed by the renewing of your mind, that you may prove what is that good, and acceptable, and perfect, will of God" (Romans 12:2).

I have been extremely fascinated by the work and research of Dr Caroline Leaf (Neuroscientist, Author and mind expert), who is also a Christian. I have spent a great deal of time learning from her seminars, sermons and interviews on-line. As a leader in her field, she explains the intricacies of neuroscience and quantum physics and how science is now catching up with ideas cited in the Bible and she does so in a way that I can understand (mostly). When talking about our thoughts she points out that 75% to 95% of all illness originates in our thought life. She refers to it as "an epidemic of toxic emotions". The average person has over 30,000 thoughts per day and if these thoughts are not controlled and filtered correctly then toxic thoughts can slip through and we create illness. Fear alone triggers 1,400 physical and chemical responses activating over 30 hormones. By consciously controlling our thought lives we can avoid such illnesses as diabetes, cancer, asthma and many more. Controlling our thoughts is the best way to detox the mind. Caroline suggests that we analyse each thought we have before deciding whether to accept or reject it. She goes on to say that our thoughts take up real estate in our brains and look like trees under the microscope. We will react to our atmosphere, whether it is life enhancing or toxic, it is our choice, if we think correctly our mind will follow. When your soul is well, you will change, you will prosper and be in health. Whatever you think about will grow, so take every thought captive and interact with the Holy Spirit, we have eternity inside of us so we have no excuses.

The way we think and choose, Caroline states in her book "The Perfect You", is the way to becoming the perfect you. We are thinking beings, made in the image of a thinking and perfect God. However, we have been given a free will, so we can choose to follow God and his way of thinking, which is for our ultimate good. We are all unique and uniquely gifted and our gifts are immutable, if we choose not to follow our divine path, no one else can do this for us. We all have a unique way of thinking and viewing the world which has been purposed by God. If we step outside of the way we are wired our whole being will suffer, we are wired for love and health, and this will be our experience if we stay on the right path. Fear and anxiety and illness are not a part of our spiritual DNA these are things we learn from allowing toxic thought into our sub-conscious minds. Healthy thoughts cause our brain to grow, healthy thoughts give us hormonal balance, healthy thinking gives us robust white blood cells to boost our immune system and avoid terminal illness. We have a much higher chance of developing illnesses if we dwell on the possibility of "generational trends" as we invite the fear of these into our thought life with all its toxicity. Worry, is the interest we pay on the trouble that is coming our way. By renewing our minds regularly and allowing healthy thoughts to dominate, we promote overall body health and wellbeing and proper food digestion; healthy thoughts lead to better skin, better cardiovascular system and on and on. Caroline has many books on this specialist subject, and extensive teaching on-line which I would fully recommend. Our thoughts then are essential to our physical, mental and spiritual health and development, and time spent harnessing and controlling this complex process is never time wasted, and will surely pay dividends further down the road.

"whatever is true, whatever is noble, whatever is

right, whatever is pure, whatever is lovely, whatever is admirable – if anything is excellent or praiseworthy – think on these things. …..whatever you have learned – put into practice and the God of peace will be with you" (Philippians 4:8-9).

3   Words of wonder or words that wound:

"What you declare and decree with your mouth shall be established" (Job 22: 28).

"Watch your thoughts, they become your words; watch your words, they become your actions; watch your actions, they become your habits; watch your habits, they become your character; watch your character, it becomes your destiny". There is much truth in this quote from Leo Tzu Taoist philosopher.

Words are free, but how you use them may cost. Words are powerful, they can build you up or tear you down, they can create and they can destroy. They can encourage or they can demoralise, they can cut and they can bring healing, they can evoke conflict or they can bring peace. God is man's supply and man can release, through his spoken word, all that belongs to him by divine right, he must however have complete faith in his spoken word.

"In the beginning was the word, and the word was with God, and the word was God. He existed in the beginning with God. Through Him all things were made, without Him nothing was made that has been made" (John 1:1). This verse of scripture refers to Jesus as "the word" and how God spoke everything into being in the story of creation, but it also emphasises the significant power of the spoken word generally, everything begins with a word. There are many examples of the power of the spoken word in the Bible, Jesus said "By your words you will be justified and by your words you will be condemned" (Mathew 12:37), "the power of life and death are in the tongue" (Proverbs 18:21). God said in the book of Isiah "my words are powerful and will not return to me void" (Isiah 55:11). We are encouraged by Jesus in Mark 11:23 to use our words with faith and to take authority over our problems in life; "I tell you the truth, if anyone says to this mountain, go, throw yourself into the sea, and does not doubt in in their heart but believes that what they say will happen, it will be done for them". Conversely our words can have a very strong negative power when used carelessly; as Charles Capps pointed out several times in his sermons, the old adage "sticks and stones may break my bones but words will never hurt me" could not be further from the truth. A person knowing the power of the word, becomes very careful of his conversations, he has to watch the reaction of his words to know that they do "not return void". Our words can be wonderful, or just as easily kill us, or be used as weapons against others if we do not guard our tongues. The apostle Paul says in the book of Ephesians 4:29, "do not let any unwholesome talk come out of your mouths, but only what is helpful for building others up according to their needs, that it may benefit those who listen"; then in the book of Colossians 3:16, "let your conversation be always full of grace, seasoned with salt, so that you may know how to answer everyone". "Keep your mouth free of perversity; keep corrupt talk far from your lips" (Proverbs 4:24). The words of the reckless pierce like swords, but the tongue of the wise brings healing.

Words have the power to build people up or confine them to where they are and cause breakdown, so it is imperative that we choose our words wisely. "Those who consider themselves religious and yet do not keep a tight rein on their tongues deceive themselves, and their religion is worthless" (James 1:26). "With the tongue we give praise to God and with the same tongue we curse those who have been made in the image and likeness of God" (James 3:9). "The word of God is alive and active, sharper than any double-edged sword, it penetrates even to dividing soul and spirit, joints and marrow, it judges the thoughts and attitudes of the heart" (Hebrews 4:12). There are in excess of 3000 references in the Bible to the importance of our words, mouth, lips and tongue so we can assume that this is a very important subject to God.

William Penn, founder of the British colony of Pennsylvania spoke of 6 principles of conversation. 1) Avoid company where it is not profitable or necessary, and on those occasions speak little, and last. 2) Silence is wisdom, where speaking is folly; and always safe. 3) Some are so foolish as to interrupt and anticipate those that speak, instead of hearing and thinking before they answer, which is uncivil. 4) If you think twice before you speak once, you will speak twice the better for it. 5) Better to say nothing than, than not to the purpose, and to speak pertinently, consider both what is fit, and when it is fit to speak. 6) In all debates, let truth be your aim, not victory or unjust interest; endeavour to gain, rather than to expose your critic. In short: never speak without thinking.

Always apply wisdom to your words and avoid using words that make others feel intimidated or inferior. Apply yourself to being an active listener rather than over talking. A gossip talks about others, a bore talks about himself but a good communicator engages in what interests you and is attentive to what you say. One of the surest signs of wisdom and maturity is to have the ability to say the right thing, in the right way, at the right time, to the right person, or, to say nothing at all. As you become wiser you speak less and say more. Everyone has the right to remain silent, so unless your words are going to be instrumental in building someone up, you should exercise this right. The Bible teaches that to answer before listening is folly and shame. It is better to keep your mouth shut and let people think you are a fool, than to open your mouth and remove all doubt. So "hold fast the form of sound words" (2 Timothy 1:13).

The book of Proverbs has much to say about our words and how we use them. "The one who has knowledge uses words with restraint, and whoever has understanding is even tempered. Even fools are thought wise if they keep silent, and discerning if they hold their tongues". (Proverbs: 17: 27-28). Then again in chapter 18 verse 2 we read "Fools find no pleasure in understanding but delight in airing their own opinions". Then verses 6-8 read as follows; "The lips of fools bring them strife, and their mouths invite a beating. The mouths of fools are their undoing, and their lips are a snare to their very lives. The words of a gossip are like choice morsels; they go down to the inmost parts". In chapter 20 we read "lips that speak knowledge are a rare jewel….. a gossip betrays confidence; so, avoid anyone who talks too much". In chapter 21 we read "Those who guard their mouths and their tongues keep themselves from calamity….a careful listener will testify successfully".

Words are made up of vibration and sound and these vibrations create our reality, a thought can only become reality by the spoken word, words have energy and power they can help and heal or hurt and humiliate. The right words said at the right time and place can alter the mind and how we view the world around us. As someone once quoted "The words you speak become the house you live in". We live in a culture where it is the norm to talk about our problems as if this will give some kind of cathartic release when actually what is happening is that we are making these problems part of our reality and the more we complain, the more we are putting negative words out into the atmosphere and this becomes truth. We must avoid using all negative words and choose what we say wisely. When we complain and moan about our situation or when we use angry or anxious words, we are not speaking in faith but rather from a place of fear and only negative outcomes will ensue. The words *utter* and *outer,* explains Catherine Ponder, have similar roots, what you utter becomes outer in your world, because of the power of words, whatever a person voices, he begins to attract. We rise and fall on the basis of our own words which we have freely chosen, we are entirely responsible for our thoughts and words. Our words govern our actions and our emotions which then lead to future actions and feelings.

Neuroscientists believe that "mental rehearsal" or repeated focus on a thought, feeling or desire, can change brain structures and influence the body. This idea was discussed in the book of Proverbs in the old testament; "my son, attend to my words, incline your ear to my sayings, let them not depart from you, for they are life to those that find them and health to all their flesh" (Proverbs 4 20-22). So repeating God's word will bring health and abundant life. We are also told that we can have what we imagine "And the Lord said, behold... nothing will be restrained from them, which they have imagined to do" (Genesis 11:6).

When we think wrongly and entertain toxic thought, we can quickly redress this and choose not to accept the thought but to reject it so it does not enter our sub-conscious mind, but once we have released spoken words, good or bad, they are out there in the ether. The tongue is a very small part of the body but can make proud boasts, it only takes a small spark and a whole forest can be burned to the ground. There are many examples in the book of James showing comparisons with the power of the tongue; the bit in the mouth of a horse will guide the whole beast, a very small rudder will steer a huge boat, despite the strong winds, and, the tongue likewise is a very small body part yet boasts great things. No human being can tame the tongue, it is a restless evil according to the book of James, for with it we bless our Lord and Father, and with it we curse people who are created in the likeness of God. The tongue is a small body part, but its power both for good and bad is completely out of proportion to its size. Proverbs 15:4 says "The soothing tongue is a tree of life, but a perverse tongue crushes the spirit". Someone once said "a fool's tongue is long enough to cut his own throat". The book of James has a lot to say about the importance of taming the tongue, "Even so the tongue is a little member, and boasts great things. Behold how great a matter a little fire can kindle! And the tongue is a fire, a world of iniquity….it defiles the whole body and sets on fire the course of nature….it is an unruly evil, full of deadly poison". God's word is spiritual law and words governed by spiritual law become a spiritual force which will work for you, just as well as idle words will work against you.

You only need to watch the power your words have on others, good or bad, to know how much effect what we say has on the hearer; you may either get the reaction of joy in their expression, or a look of being completely crestfallen. Our words carry vibrations, and, whatever we say we begin to attract, so we must be ever mindful and cautious in our choice of words. Florence Scovel Shinn in her book "The Game of Life and How to Play it" mentioned an old saying that a man only dares use his words for three purposes, to "heal, bless or prosper" because what a man says of others will be said of him and what he wishes for others, he will be wishing for himself, curses like chickens come home to roost.

Our bodies can be transformed by the spoken word and disease can be completely removed from our consciousness. To heal the body, we have to first heal the soul so we must choose life with our thoughts and words. We have the power to affect our lives for the better by the words we choose, we can change our sickness for divine health and replace our lack and limitation with God's prosperity. When we speak, the words we use impress upon the subconscious mind and becomes our external reality. People make their worst mistakes by speaking to others when angry or upset as there is so much negativity behind their words which sends out negative vibration and results in negative reality. People who are constantly talking about their infirmities are often the ones who are regularly unwell. Given the power our words hold, it would be useful every time we are about to complain or say something negative to others, to ask ourselves why we are about to say this and how it will help us or make us happy; we need to taste our words before we spit them out. When we analyse what we are about to say in this way it quickly reveals to us whether we are speaking out of love or fear. If we are speaking negatively, due to feeling hard done to or unworthy, we will only add to this feeling by using such words, and compound the larger issues at the root of our underlying emotions.

It is so harmful to our mind and body to use such statements as "I'm afraid I can't", or "that makes me sick" or "I was worried to death". What we are doing here is we are affirming negative circumstances in our lives in the present and in the future. Making such affirmations come from a source of fear and will only attract more of the same, anxiety breeds anxiety, we attach fearful and doubting emotions to these words and allow a foothold for the enemy to use. It doesn't matter whether we consciously, and literally believe what we are saying, we are putting these words out there with the negative energy that they embody, and as mentioned in the previous chapters, thoughts become things if regularly given attention.

Our spoken words are creative forces, which are picked up by the inner ear, and signals are sent to the brain. On the subject of ears, how many ears did Davy Crockett have?.......the answer is 3, a left ear, a right ear and a wild frontier, I couldn't resist. When we desire something earnestly, we begin to speak it out, and by so doing we are both affirming our desires to the universe and releasing energy to this, and we are also reaffirming our desires to ourselves and establishing patterns of belief in our subconscious minds. By regularly repeating such positive affirmation our spoken words become our reality. We can use our words in all life situations to attain the results we are hoping to achieve, for our health, finances, relationships etc. "Words and thoughts are a tremendous vibratory force, ever moulding man's body and affairs" (Florence Scovel Shinn).

"In the long run, the sharpest weapon of all is a kind and gentle spirit" (Anne Frank).

So, assuming that in the main we are able to some degree to harness and filter our thoughts and only speak what we intend, using the right temperament, how then do we actively pursue dreams and fulfil our destiny. We need to firstly decide what it is we want to do with our lives, what do we mostly think about, talk about and get excited about, what gets us out of bed in the morning. Our individual gifting has been described as the thing we are most passionate about, the thing we would most like to be involved in if we could make a living out of it, the area we are good at, and where we feel we have much to offer to others. Once we have ascertained what our gifting is, which should be very obvious to most of us, we need then to then pursue this with hunger and passion, as if failing to succeed in our quest is simply not an option. Our personal success and ultimate prosperity will be waiting for us, universal attributes are in place and will support our thoughts, words and actions, "the universe is a friendly place……God does not play dice with the universe" (Albert Einstein).

4 Prosperity within:

Let us throw off everything that hinders and entangles, and let us run with perseverance the race marked out for us (Hebrews 12:1)

There is a spiritual side to prosperity, and the common thread amongst wealthy and successful people is often referred to as "prosperity consciousness". This is referring to the paradigm of viewing your entire life and situation through a lens of prosperity within your thought processes. Having a prosperity consciousness means that a person has the assurance of an infinite supply of all the elements of prosperity; love, peace, happiness, health, wealth, but it is our responsibility to ask for and receive this in our personal reality. Scripture tells us that we have not because we ask not, we serve a covenant God who granted us free will and He can do nothing for us to change our situations without our asking. Kat Kerr author of the Revealing Heaven books says we should "ask for and receive abundant grace for each day" and to do this first thing in the morning as we wake. We live under divine intelligence and God is our source and provider but we need to ask and engage our thoughts, knowing that when we ask, we receive. We are told this principle many times in the Bible, "ask, and it shall be given unto you, seek and you will find, knock and the door will be opened, (Mathew 7:7).

A person with a prosperity mindset knows implicitly that divine substance holds an abundance of happiness, wealth, opportunity, health and wisdom etc, so we must manage our control of this immense power to our good, and we do this with our thoughts and then affirm with our words. When we think on purpose about our prosperity our default setting should be "I have all I need and more", "I will fulfil my destiny", "my God shall supply all my needs according to his riches in glory".

Some Christians take issue with a prosperity

mindset and believe that it is wrong to want more, that we should be happy with our lot, this of course is completely unscriptural. There are many verses in the Bible which clearly affirm Gods interest in His people's prosperity. "Keep this book of the Law always on your lips; meditate on it day and night, so that you may be careful to do everything written in it. Then you will be prosperous and successful" (Joshua 1:8). "Beloved I wish above all things that you may prosper in all things and be in health, even as your soul prospers" (3 John: 2).

By maintaining that God plays no part in your financial success, you are making your success purely your own achievement which would constitute pride. To prosper in all things means exactly that, your family, health, wellbeing, career and finances. God wants you to succeed in life and wants you to have all the things you need to get there. In the Old Testament God said keep the words of this covenant and do them, that you may prosper in all you do" (Deuteronomy 29:9). Then in the New Testament Jesus said "Seek first the kingdom of God and His righteousness, and all these things will be added unto you" (Mathew 6:33). God has given you His authority and creative ability to succeed in anything He calls you to do. "But remember the

Lord your God, for it is He who gives you the ability to produce wealth" (Deuteronomy 8:18). If you have any area of doubt about the intention of God to bless and prosper His people then take a look at the list of blessings for obedience listed in Deuteronomy 28:1-14). As Dale Carnegie once said "success is getting what you want, happiness is wanting what you get". Be sure to keep to your calling, it's a journey that will bring happiness if you stick to your assignment.

Our thinking must be positive at all times and, if we slip, and entertain any thought of lack or limitation we straight away bring our thoughts back to what is lovely and of good report, we hold the wisdom of ages inside. We need to be consistent, persistent, diligent, fervent, peaceable, calm, grateful and thankful in our thoughts and affirmations. Since ancient times there has been a clear understanding that our lives and the circumstances around us are external manifestations of our thoughts and feelings, so therefore a product of our conscious and sub-conscious thought activity. When looking at the money paradigm held by the rich and the poor in society there is a clear disparity, the rich person has a blueprint of abundance in his sub-conscious mind while the poor person still sees lack and limitation as his lot due to embedded thought processes around "I can't afford it", "we will never have enough" etc. The universe, however, is lavish and eternally abundant and there is much more than enough for everyone and for always if people would only tap into this rich supply. Affirming in our thoughts that our source is abundant and available to us at all times brings peace and builds up our faith, conversely focussing on lack and limitation engenders fear, the opposite of faith, and brings insecurity, greed, hoarding and anxiety. A prosperity minded person will constantly sow good thoughts in order to reap their abundance, our prosperity mindset will emerge from constantly sowing abundant thoughts into our sub-conscious mind and always thinking positively on things of good report.

Abundance is a flow of energy and we can have whatever we desire but to do so we must change our ideas about money and be prepared to receive as well as to give and we should always give to others more value than the abundance we receive. We are meant to be prosperous and to fulfil our destiny so we need to be excited and passionate about this and affirm "I am the best person for the job" no one can run our race better than we can, we just need to be on the right path and frequency to breakthrough and reprogram the old paradigms. Don't look at the problems in life but look at solutions. Jesus said "Truly I tell you, if anyone says to this mountain, go throw yourself into the sea, and does not doubt in their heart but believes that what they say will happen, it will be done for them" (Mark 11:23). We need to get into the divine flow and invest time and dedication, and join with the forces of nature in taking control of our futures. Everything that happens to you is a reflection of what you believe about yourself. It is impossible to draw to ourselves more than we think we are worth. So how we see ourselves determines our relationships with others and our outlook on life. We must maintain a strong self-belief and not be dependent on others to determine who we are. We must be ever grateful for all our blessings and give thanks no matter how small a thing may be. We must be constantly ready to learn, "if you are not willing to learn, no one can help you. If you are determined to learn, no one can stop you" (Zig Ziglar). The Bible tells us in Hosea 4:6, "my people perish for their lack of knowledge".

Dr Joe Dispenza has made ground breaking steps in his research into how people can change their lives for the better by using focussed thought process. His research is applicable to improving health, relationships, creativity, wealth and all aspects of prosperity. Dr Dispenza has written several books on this topic and has many fascinating seminars and discussion sessions on You tube. Joe suggests that we need to stop our thoughts from being equal to our emotions, because this means that nothing is changing and we are living from past experience. When we begin to have clear intention and vision of what we desire (which already exists in the quantum field), and we begin to think about what it would be like to be wealthy, or loved or well, the frontal lobe of the brain gets involved. The frontal lobe pulls together all the neurones from past experience to create an ideal, this is a potential experience that awaits us. Dr Dispenza goes on to say that thoughts are the language of the mind and feelings are the language of the body so we must also emotionally embrace this desired future before it manifests. We need also to give thanks for what we want before it materialises, at this point it is a possibility in the quantum field. Our sub-conscious mind then begins to think it is living in this reality and we are beginning to create a new state of being.

As a key point in the Law of Attraction we need to harness our thoughts and direct them accordingly, choosing whether to accept or reject them and then to purposefully direct them into our sub-conscious mind. Our thoughts are highly creative and are the origin of all things, we live in a universe that will reflect our mental climate and join with us to create our future; we have a choice to make, do we want a future of lack or prosperity. Thoughts become things! mind is over matter, so we need to think on purpose and choose life, health, wealth, peace, perfect creative and spiritual expression. When any negative thoughts invade our mental space, we must immediately dismiss these thoughts and reject them and use positive affirmation to replace any such thoughts of lack or negativity with thoughts of success and abundance; "I am a spiritual magnet attracting only that which is for my highest good". Any negative feelings we harbour of grievance, doubt or failure, any restlessness or frustration will make us suffer; deal with such negativity swiftly and move on. Our ships can only come in after we have sent them out, we must be open vessels, calm and clear for the universe to fill us up with divine intuition and spiritual creativity; "our ships come in on a calm sea" (Florence Scovel Shinn).

In terms of our prosperity, we must give conscious direction to our thought processes and have a definiteness of purpose, or, as many prosperity authors would say we need to have a "dominant thought" and when we are specific and detailed and we affirm our dominant thought processes into our sub-conscious mind we have immense power and control and our sub-conscious mind will eventually accept these thoughts as reality, which in turn will then manifest in our lives.

Both poverty and wealth are born out of thought, but 'successful people don't find time, they make time' to succeed, we are limited only by our imagination.

"The privilege of a lifetime is being who you are" (Joseph Campbell). We are individually unique, not dependent on others, we are fearfully and wonderfully made, we are exactly and precisely who we are intended to be, a one-of-a-kind creation for which there is no comparison. Nothing is impossible, "impossible is for the unwilling" (John Keats). Each day of your life was scheduled and planned before you experienced a single one of them (Psalm 139:16), it is now time to begin walking them out with child-like dreams and imagination and with the determination to fulfil your destiny. See each day as a new opportunity to develop and hone your craft. Problems will arise but when they do don't see them as burdensome forces of opposition but as opportunities to grow, learn, improve and adjust so that you are better off after the problem than before it first existed. "No problem can be solved from the same level of consciousness that created it" (Einstein); take problems apart, strip them back and use them as stepping stones to greater things.

"A smooth sea never made a skilled sailor" (Franklin D Roosevelt).. try and try again.

5 I am grateful:

"It's not happy people who are grateful. Its grateful people who are happy"

"Be thankful in all circumstances, for this is God's will for you" (1 Thessalonians 5:18). This is a commandment, not an idea, and there are more commandments in scripture about thanksgiving than anything else. God likes people to be always thankful, just as we would like our children to always say thank you.

"Learn to be thankful for what you already have, while you pursue all that you want" (Jim Rohn).

Gratitude changes your focus to what you have, not what you are missing and wires your brain for increased productivity. Gratitude connects you with your innate ability to create happiness and prosperity in your life enabling you to see the beauty, and good in things, which will then be reflected in your own reality, this will then be self-perpetuating. If you are thankful for what you have, you will end up having more. Gratitude leads to greatness and counting your blessings will surely bring more blessings your way.

Gratefulness and thankfulness are keys to spiritual connectivity, when we exercise these elements we join with infinite intelligence and kick start our faith into shifting gear. There has been much written about the Laws of Attraction and gratitude is a very important part of this process but people often neglect this element or at least not give it the importance and priority it should have as a life transforming component. Gratitude is arguably the most important law of attraction and when practiced can immediately transform all areas of your life, if you want to be happy, find gratitude. Gratitude brings dividends in all areas of our lives, not only bringing financial wealth but also increasing our spiritual, mental, social and physical well-being and enrichment.

Being grateful has significant power to raise a person's vibration bringing us into aligned frequency with the energy of the universe. "Gratitude is an attitude that hooks us up to our source of supply and the more grateful you are, the closer you are to your maker, the architect of the universe, to the spiritual core of your being" (Bob Proctor). Gratitude has been defined as 'great attitude' which when used in a heart-felt manner will unlock the abundant treasures of the universe. We all know how it feels when someone shows us gratitude as opposed to criticism and judgement, gratitude holds within it healing, peace, growth and self-worth. Those who live in lack are usually the people who do not express gratitude for what they have and so do not attract more, in fact they perpetuate their lack. The lack of gratitude in your life can perpetuate a state of dissatisfaction and unfulfillment which in turn, will attract more of the same, conversely, making the shift to being ever grateful, will quickly draw positivity and enable your focus to move to an abundant life rather than one of lack. Instead of wasting valuable time complaining and moaning about life circumstances, time is better spent being thankful for your situation and all that you have as this instantly shifts your vibration and allows you to begin the process of manifesting your dreams.

"Gratitude is the healthiest of all human emotions. The more you express gratitude for what you have, the more likely you will have even more to express gratitude for" (Zig Ziglar - Author). There is always something to be grateful for and when we verbally express this our lives will begin to improve. Gratitude is the opposite of complaining, and just as complaining brings with it lack and sickness and stress, gratitude brings love, health and abundance. There are around 1200 different chemicals that come into play to nourish and restore the body when we are in a state of gratitude.

We are connected to the creative power and energy of the universe which is limitless and so our future prosperity also has no limit, we should be forever grateful and thankful for the potential at our disposal. Gratitude can transform lives quickly and produce great results, being grateful embodies a passion more than all other laws, it is on a very high frequency and the universe will join in with the energy you are creating and will bless you in return. Be grateful for the small things in life and also be grateful for the things you are about to receive or would like to receive, be it happiness, health or material assets. Gratitude gives added energy to your faith when you make your affirmations and call the things to you that are not yet seen, it tells the universe that these things are yours before you receive them making the whole process flow more freely.

Saying thanks regularly throughout your day is empowering for you and for those around you, it puts us in true alignment to receive. It is a good use of time, do this in the morning and be thankful for what the day holds for you and for what you do not yet see, but wish to see. Then again at night it is good practice to look back on the day and be grateful for what the day brought to us no matter how small or significant that may be. When you thank God in advance for that which you choose to experience in your reality, you, in effect, acknowledge that it is already there. Gratitude is a feeling or attitude in acknowledgement of a benefit that one has received or will receive and spans many religions in terms of being an important component. "Thankfulness is thus the most powerful statement to God; an affirmation that even before you ask, I have answered. Therefore, never supplicate, Appreciate" (Neale Donald Walsch – Conversations with God: an uncommon Dialogue). This is a fascinating, humbling and mind-blowing phenomena that God hears us before we put our requests to Him. "And it shall come to pass, that before they call, I will answer, and while they are yet speaking, I will hear (Isaiah 65: 24).

We need to have clear and detailed ideas of what our desires are but we must not worry or be concerned in anyway about how we will get to our goals. The universe will work with us and create synergy, causing situations and events to take place that will work together for our good if we are operating on the right frequency. We are to expect the unexpected and not try to rationalise the supernatural. Being grateful prior to seeing a situation come into play is very powerful and is a necessary leap of faith on this journey. We need to feel and experience the heightened level of emotion that comes with the outcome before it becomes physical reality, we need to be living in this future experience, viewing our situation from the vantage point of the outcome, back over. What we are giving thanks for already exists in the quantum field, it's just not a part of our reality yet, we are in effect moving from cause and effect to causing an effect as Joe Dispenza states, we are changing what is inside us to produce something outside. Gratitude sends out a signal that something has already happened, it is more than just thought, it is the feeling that we already have fulfilment of our dominant thoughts and desires. Our bodies which only understand feelings will then begin to believe that that this is happening in our reality now. Everything is energy as Einstein said and it is interconnected across time and space, the quantum field holds all probabilities which we can collapse in our reality through our thoughts and feelings.

When we use gratitude, we are showing our heart-felt appreciation for both things we have and also for things we are believing for, and by doing this we are also affirming that we deserve these things and that God will give us the things we ask for when we ask believing. "Whatever you ask for in prayer, believe that you have received it, and it will be yours" (Mark 11:24). Theologian John Henry Jowett said, "Every virtue, if divorced from thankfulness, is maimed and limps along the spiritual road". Without gratitude your faith becomes a hollow religious practice and your love for others fades, leaving you drained and devoid of happiness. Gratitude, transforms overwhelmed strugglers into triumphant conquerors, and its transforming power is reserved for those who know and acknowledge the giver of every good gift.

If a person has abundance but does not have

gratitude, they will often ultimately lose the abundance they had. Conversely if a person shows great gratitude for what he has but lacks abundance, the universe will see this gratitude and will provide more of what this person wishes. "Gratitude can transform common days into joy, and change ordinary opportunities into blessings" (William Arthur Ward). Gratitude can turn what you have into more than enough and bring order, clarity and peace to our day. The easiest way to make blessings count, is to count your blessings, because whatever you appreciate and give attention to will grow. "When I started counting my blessings, my whole life turned around" (Willie Nelson).

Thank You for life, thank You for clean air, thank You for sight, thank You for being there. Thanks for the fells and the falls between them, and how the woodland smells when the pine's in season. I love the morning dew, when the dawn is breaking, and I think of You while the world is waking. All Your creation, what can I say, prayers for tomorrow, thanks for today. (P. Cawley *Thankyou*)

We need to make the practice of gratitude a habit, setting aside specific time, in the morning, being thankful for what is to come "thanks in advance", or at bedtime, to be thankful for what the day brought to us. Being grateful in the morning can have added benefits as it puts the day into perfect vibrational frequency which will then attract to us what we have been giving attention to.

As mentioned earlier, it's not happy people who are thankful, its thankful people who are happy. "When you are grateful fear disappears and abundance appears" (Tony Robbins).

Gratitude is a shift in thought, instead of being bogged down in the stresses of everyday life and business, take some time to count your blessings. Try coming up with 3 new things each day to be grateful for. It is a habit, and like all habits it takes practice and discipline to develop, but is time very well spent. Gratitude is not just for good times it also makes dealing with difficult times a lot easier as well. Affirming at the beginning of each day what you are grateful for sets your day off to a wholesome start and puts you as a human being in harmony with creation around you, being thankful puts you in the correct vibrational frequency to receive more as you are at one with the universe around you.

"I am grateful for my God, Jesus Blood and my

salvation
The Holy Spirit and the Word, my life and all creation
I am grateful for my health, and my kin, and for faith from within
I am grateful for Your love, You guide me all the way
I am thankful for Your power, and my Divine connection
I am thankful for Your death and for Your resurrection
I am blessed with Your abundant grace, to run this race
I am thankful for Your grace and mercies everyday" (P Cawley *Grateful*)

6 Humble Pie: (RDA one large slice every day- custard optional)

"Humble yourselves therefore under God's mighty hand, that He may lift you up in due time" (1 Peter 5:6).

Humility is often referred to as a lack of arrogance and genuine gratitude, or taking a modest view of one's importance. At first the quality of being humble can be mistaken as a negative quality, as a sign of weakness rather than a virtue of strength; but it is in fact one of the most powerful human attributes of growth.

Humility is widely seen as a virtue which centres on low self-preoccupation, or unwillingness to put oneself forward, so the complete opposite of narcissism, it can also imply the characteristic of being grounded. "Humility is in essence, not thinking less of yourself but rather thinking of yourself less" (C S Lewis).

We know from scripture that God resists the proud and gives grace to the humble, so we need to be pursuing life without arrogant and selfish pride. The book of Proverbs tells us that with pride comes disgrace, but with humility comes wisdom and that humility comes before honour. Humility is the fear of the Lord; its wages are riches and honour and life. There are many verses in scripture which emphasise how important the virtue of Humility is in a person's life. "Do nothing out of selfish ambition or vain conceit, rather in humility value others above yourselves, not looking to your own interests, but each of you to the interests of the others" (Philippians 2:3-4). "For those who exalt themselves will be humbled and those who humble themselves will be exalted" (Mathew 23:12). Christianity puts great emphasis on humility which was demonstrated quintessentially by Jesus who came as a servant to mankind and humbled himself by giving His life for the sake others despite who He is. "God opposes the proud but gives grace to the humble" (James 4:6). "When pride comes, then comes disgrace, but with the humble is wisdom" (Proverbs 11:2). "The fear of the Lord is instruction in wisdom, and humility comes before honour" (Proverbs 15:33). "If my people who are called by my name humble themselves, and pray and seek my face and turn from their wicked ways, then I will hear from heaven and will forgive their sin and heal their land" (2 Chronicles 7: 14). "For everyone who exalts himself will be humbled, and he who humbles himself will be exalted" (Luke 14: 11). "Do nothing from rivalry or conceit, but in humility count others more significant than yourselves" (Philippians 2: 3). "Towards the scorners he is scornful, but to the humble he gives favour" (Proverbs 3 :34). "He leads the humble in what is right, and teaches the humble his way" (Psalm 25: 9). "Seek the Lord, all you humble of the land, who do his just commands, seek righteousness; seek humility" (Zephaniah 2: 3). "Whoever humbles himself like a child is the greatest in the kingdom of heaven" (Mathew 18: 4).

Humility begins when we empty ourselves, when we realise that we are, of ourselves, not entitled to anything, but rather that there is something bigger than ourselves looking down on us. "The only true wisdom is in knowing we know nothing" (Socrates). Emptying ourselves engenders honesty in regard to who we are within our environment, by practicing humility we know the reality of who we are and this in essence is the beginning of wisdom. Humility helps a person care less about who is wrong and who is right and that you, and everyone around you can always find room for improvement. Humility stops you from taking things for granted and helps you to treat others in the way they ought to be treated. Humility teaches us that we don't know everything so we become curious, ask questions and begin to learn. The more we learn as we follow this process, the closer we get to creating the life we want for ourselves and our family. "The more you know, the more humble you become" (Albert Einstein). In a search for wisdom the humble person does not mind where the revelation comes from, being proved wrong is of little consequence, as it is just another opportunity to learn. Humility breeds gratitude and when you are grateful you will attract more of the things you are grateful for. When you humble yourself, you see more clearly the value of others, thus creating a happier and more trusting society. "Life's most persistent and urgent question is, what are you doing for others" (Martin Luther King Jr).

Nelson Mandela once said "The first thing is to be honest with yourself. You can never have an impact on society if you have not changed yourself...great peacemakers are all people of integrity, of honesty and humility". One definition of humility is having the feeling or attitude that you have no special importance that makes you better than others.

Humility is an asset for self-improvement, it helps you to see the areas of your life that may be in need of improvement. This is definitely true of our inner well-being. Adopting a stance of humility will make a person far more resilient; if you can admit and acknowledge where you go wrong, you can learn and instigate positive change rather than becoming angry and frustrated when perceived failure comes. Humility is not just about acknowledging weaknesses but also recognising your strengths and then using those assets to become a better person. Humility begins with accepting who we are and what makes us human. Those who walk in humility often show greater generosity, helpfulness and gratitude, which are all qualities that will only serve to draw us closer to others. Humble people tend to have many qualities in common; they tend to be aware of their surroundings, keep good relationships, make difficult decisions easily, put others before themselves, are good listeners, are curious, will speak honestly, say thank you, have an abundance mindset, will often start sentences with you, not I, will readily accept feedback, will assume responsibility and ask for help when needed. Humble people are filled with gratitude, will acknowledge that they don't have all the answers but will strive to add value to others. "Admit when you're wrong; shut up when you're right" (John Gottman).

Research has shown that humble people tend to have an accurate view of themselves, they are able to acknowledge their mistakes and limitations and are open and accommodating to the ideas and viewpoints of others. They will keep their own accomplishments and abilities in perspective, have a low self-focus and appreciate the value of all things including other people. A person's level of humility will show in not constantly trying to impress, recognising the things you can do and the things you cannot do so well; making time for others to express themselves, and actively listening to them, and not being judgmental to others. "Do not judge. Or you too will be judged, and with the same measure you use, it will be measured against you" (Mathew 7: 1-2). According to the Bible, humility is a very powerful thing on so many levels and will reap benefits in many areas of our lives. If we are humble, we will not grow weary, we will be saved from affliction, we will be open to receive guidance and teaching, we will be given grace, wisdom and honour, we will be lifted up.

Being humble then is trying to be the best you can with no jealousy of the fortunes of others, not feeling in anyway threatened or worried about the actions of others. Humble people are not in competition with others but rather will encourage and invest in others whilst remaining confident on their journey to their own destiny. They acknowledge that everyone has the potential to be great and to excel in their given area, as greatness is a choice and a right to all who embrace it. Some of the greatest historical figures of all time lived a life of humility, with the greatest example by far being Jesus. A person can be humble or exalt themselves, it is a lifestyle choice. History shows that we are not naturally humble, survival instinct throughout history has taught us to put self, first. It is therefore clearly a personal choice to overcome our nature and instead be humble. Make the right choice then, it will be of benefit to you in all areas of your life and longevity, humility is wisdom. "The only wisdom we can hope to acquire is the wisdom of humility: humility is endless" (TS Elliot).

7 Forgive to live:

Gratitude fosters true forgiveness and puts you on a platform where you can sincerely say without condemnation or regret, "I forgive you" and then glean wisdom from the life lesson you have experienced, this puts things back into perspective and brings peace on the subject and hope for new beginnings. You can then move forward "Forgetting what is behind and straining towards what is ahead" (Philippians 3:13). Forgiveness is crucial if you are to successfully get beyond the hurt of a situation, whether you have been cheated on, or lied to, wrongly accused or abused, you must forgive and let it go. Choosing to continue life, carrying offense and bitterness will just keep the wound festering. Not everyone belongs in your life, and everyone has the right not to want to pursue a relationship with another person. Horses for courses, some relationships were never meant to be, for your own good, or for mutual preservation. Whatever the issue, forgive quickly, as God forgives you. Don't seek punishment for the other person, a grudge is very heavy to carry. Bitterness is poison to your body and may manifest negatively either through emotional or physical health.

"And when you stand praying, if you hold anything against anyone, forgive them, so that your Father in heaven may forgive you." (Mark 11:25). "Then Peter came to Jesus and asked, Lord, how many times should I forgive my brother who sins against me? Up to seven times? And Jesus said no, seventy times seven" (Mathew 18: 21).

The importance of forgiveness as a pre-curser to any acts of faith being successful cannot be emphasised enough; it is crucial to physical and spiritual health and well-being. Forgive others and God will forgive you. Forgiveness is part of the law of Gratitude, we cannot be grateful and be using positive self-talk and affirmation whilst still harbouring unforgiveness as one will negate the other.

Forgiveness is for our own growth and continued happiness, if we hold on to hurt and pain or any offense or resentment it causes anger and frustration and it will ultimately hurt us more than it harms the offender. Forgiveness brings freedom and allows us to be able to move on without harbouring any judgement. Christians are called to forgive 70 x 7 which is symbolic of an infinite number of times as this is congruent with the endless number of times God forgives His people.

We are instructed in Ephesians 4:31 - 32 to get rid of all bitterness, rage and anger, brawling and slander and every form of malice, and rather be kind and compassionate to one another, tender hearted, forgiving each other just as god forgave you. In the book of Hebrews 12:14-15 we read "Pursue peace with all people, and holiness, without which no one will see the Lord. Looking carefully lest anyone fall short of the grace of God, lest any root of bitterness springing up cause trouble, and by this many become defiled".

When we do what God says it does us good, it is

neuroprotective, we get physical benefits from being kind, forgiving and caring to others. The *law of entanglement,* or the law of relationships in quantum physics states that relationship is the defining characteristic of everything in space and time. Everyone and everything is linked and we all have an effect on each other independent of distance (Dr Caroline Leaf – Switch on Your Brain). Caroline notes a biblical correlation here, "so we, being many, are one body in Christ, and individually members one of another" (Romans 12:5). She goes on to say if you are not doing what God put you on earth to do, your divine sense of purpose, then you will affect the lives of others, as we are all part of God and are interconnected. Our intentions, prayers, and words or feelings towards others will have impact on their lives. We are so entangled with others that our intentions alter our DNA and that of others that we are involved with. What we say and do to others good or bad will have a physiological effect on us and on them. We know that thoughtful reassurance builds us up and we also know how we feel when someone is slanderous or hurtful towards us.

Forgiveness then is crucial and will have a bearing on our whole journey towards prosperity and fulfilling our destiny. Every disease is caused by a mind not at ease, and unforgiveness is the most prolific cause according to Florence Shinn, she said just as "constant criticism will cause rheumatism, unforgiveness will harden arteries or the liver and also affect eye-sight", amongst many other ailments. We are taught to love our neighbours as ourselves and to demonstrate good will towards mankind but unfortunately our biggest battle is not with the devil but with ourselves. We must always remember that we have the power of life and death, blessing and cursing, what are we going to choose?

Forgiveness is getting rid of resentment and bitterness from our bodies and as we get rid of toxicity, we get rid of disease from our bodies. Caroline states that although we cannot control life events, we can control how we react to them, hanging on to hurt and bearing grudges is toxic and all such harboured bitterness will make us vulnerable to ill health. If you have not forgiven a person you are connected to, that person, and yourself will be suffering in body, soul or spirit regardless of proximity. Without forgiveness the toxic thoughts will germinate between you and the person who wronged you. When we forgive, we release ourselves from the hurt that was done to us and only then can we free our minds. We must replace toxic thoughts with healthy ones and dwell on positive thinking, take every thought captive and renew our minds daily with the word of God. You need to forgive the person then hand it over to God so it is released from your body, and the bible says "He will repay with retribution those who trouble you" (2 Thessalonians 1:6). It takes great courage to forgive someone who has hurt you but we must make this choice and let the healing process begin.

To reference scripture again the most obvious example of the importance of forgiveness has to be the reference made in the Lord's Prayer (Mathew 6:9-13). Here we see in priority order how we should pray. We are told to first lift up the name of God the Father and then we may proceed with our requests to God; interestingly it is immediately after asking for our daily sustenance that we should then ask for forgiveness for our trespasses, so that we can forgive those who trespass against us, this takes priority over our plea for help in resisting temptation and wrong doing. By definition this must mean that that we are not eligible to be delivered from sin and temptation until we have first asked for forgiveness, and then forgiven those who have done us wrong. In verse 14 and 15 of this chapter this is further emphasised, stating that if you forgive others you will be forgiven by the Father, but if you do not forgive others, then neither will your Father in heaven forgive you. Malcolm Baxter in his book "Be the Head and Not the Tail" states that our joy and happiness in life can be significantly compromised if we harbour unforgiveness. He states "we open the door for Satan to attack us, and because God's word has been spoken, He cannot save us in this life (if we choose to ignore His word)". We may needlessly suffer ill health, broken relationships, financial insecurity, accidents etc. God does not want this suffering to fall on us but He gave us free will and we have choices to make, we are instructed to choose life.

Holding in anger, resentment and unforgiveness, or holding grudges against others will upset our own homeostasis, and, musing on angry thoughts can manifest into physical pain, disease and illness like stress, blood pressure, and poor immunity to name but a few. We must forgive to be freed from the ties that bind us to our illness and pain.

8 Affirmation ignites creation:

Affirmations are positive statements that describe a desire or a goal we aspire to achieve, these affirmations are to be used on a regular basis with repetition and an investment of emotion in order to impress them upon the sub-conscious mind. Affirmations are repeated statements spoken out with full confidence about a perceived truth, which over time helps to reshape the assumptions and beliefs a person may have about themselves and those around them. By changing their internal environment, a person can then shape their external reality, the only limitations here are those imposed by the individual themselves. Repeating affirmations consciously is one of our most powerful tools for healing the body, mind, heart and spirit. "You will also decree a thing and it will be established for you" (Job 22: 28).

The sub-conscious mind cannot tell reality from affirmed desire and when we make affirmations in faith, with feeling, it triggers the sub-conscious mind to begin to work to find a spiritual equivalent, securing and creating associated events and situations into our lives. Our conscious mind begins this process and then the sub-conscious mind takes over, we influence our sub-conscious and in turn transform our habits, behaviour and attitude. We need to be methodical and consistent with affirmations, having full belief that our desires are becoming truth. We must make our affirmations in the present tense, if your desire is to be healthy than affirm something like "I am healthy and well and my fitness increases daily", the sub-conscious mind will recognise this, and work overtime to make this happen now. We must see and feel that our desires are real and present regardless of the current situation and this attracts it into our lives.

Daily positive affirmations as a life style tool, spoken out loud, allow a person to hear with their inner ear, the words resonate and settle into the sub-conscious mind, imprinting and creating change. Our thoughts have huge impact on what we manifest in our lives but our words hold the real and determining power. We confirm to the universe how we see ourselves, our circumstances and how we see others. We affirm our desires and dreams and we define who we are to ourselves and to all around us. Daily affirmation puts us in vibrational alignment for abundance rather than lack and gets us to our goals much quicker. Self-affirming also keeps us more guarded about our thought lives, helping us avoid negativity and keeping us on track with our dominant thoughts and our journey towards fulfilling our desires. Positive affirmation also keeps us in connection with feelings of gratitude which further enhances the process. The optimistic nature of this process has also proved to have many health benefits and so could increase our longevity.

When doing your daily affirmations always use the present tense, do not affirm a wish or a hope and never use any form of negative affirmation like "I would like less illness in my life", rather, affirm "I am fit and well, I am strong and well able". When making our affirmations we need to begin to feel the accomplishment of what we are affirming and fully invest our emotions in this, it is a good idea to set aside a specific time for affirmation and visualisation and incorporate it into your morning meditation or devotional time in a quiet and comfortable place.

The words "I am" are two of the most powerful words within our vocabulary and how we then end the sentence will define who we are to ourselves and to those around us, speaking in this way will both change chemicals within the body and begin to create our future reality. When we say I am, we are creating/recreating ourselves depending on what follows these two words. We are creating powerful energy and putting this energy out into the quantum field and we will begin to establish our reality either positive or negative. The frontal lobe of the brain will begin to scan the brain for experiences and past knowledge and the associated feelings and emotions and we begin to form new chemicals and neuro-pathways and "neurons that fire together wire together" as previously quoted. Be sure to affirm positive "I am" statements; I am secure, I am radiant, I am vibrant, I am trusting etc and not to fall into the trap of casually affirming things like I am fragile, frustrated, irritated, aggravated or irritable. Use affirmations like I am strong, I am safe, I am loyal, I am fulfilled, I am loved, I am fit and healthy, I am wealthy, I am patient, I am kind, etc.

The power of affirmation is significant and not without scientific and psychological backing from research. Self-affirmation has been shown to significantly reduce stress, to motivate people into more physical activity and better lifestyle to help people succeed in dieting, to boost morale and self-confidence. To increase self-belief bringing motivation to aspire to better careers and higher earnings, to improve relationships and increase wellbeing and general happiness in life. Affirmation helps to develop and encourage a more optimistic outlook on life and reducing negativity; a positive outlook goes a long way to avoiding many stress related illnesses and diseases.

The Bible has much to say about affirmation and speaking the word of scripture this has been fully discussed in chapter 4. Turn back to refresh on this.

9 Visualise to materialise:

If you ask God, He will give you a vision for your life purpose enabling you to see the end result and fill you with passion and excitement as you work towards achieving this goal. Visualisation gives you a bigger perspective, it expands your view of your future and highlights what you believe you are able to achieve.

Visualisation is a natural ability we all possess, our minds will naturally work in a series of pictures. Visualisation as a technique helps to imprint our desires and dreams into the sub-conscious mind and we begin to live the reality of our dreams before they actually come into fruition. When we visualise, we are fabricating images in our minds, we are not using sight but rather we are cultivating our imagination, we are using our thoughts which generate specific vibration, and as mentioned in chapter two our thoughts become things. It is important to remember that when we are using visualisation, we need to be fully invested bringing all our sensory awareness into play. In the process of visualisation, we need to see ourselves living and being in the situation that we desire, how does it feel and smell, what sounds are around you and what colours come into play. See yourself as the main participant within what you visualise. Affirmation can be brought into your visualisation, so whilst visualising yourself in your dream house you can be affirming "I am successful and wealthy and can easily afford the lifestyle I am visualising". When visualising your dreams, go big, don't be conservative in your desires, you must trust the process and know that imprinting these desires within your sub-conscious mind will ultimately bring them into your reality. When you use visualisation techniques be sold out in the moment. Invest fully your senses and emotions, be clear and detailed to get the best results. Full concentration is required but you need to be in a relaxed frame of mind to allow your imagination to fully explore all possibilities you are investing in. I must emphasise again the need to fully invest emotionally, feel the joy and happiness that the new situation will bring, picture yourself enjoying the experience and exercise immense gratitude as the vision unfolds.

The tools of visualisation vary but will include elements of quiet contemplation and meditation, regular focus on the components that make up your vision as you journey towards fulfilling your destiny. Vision boards can be extremely useful to help to create focus, these should include words and images that make up your overarching desires and dreams. It may be useful to have several vision boards around the house as visual reminders of what you are aiming for, this may include your ideal home, car, body image, holiday or whatever is important within your vision.

What do you truly want, you must feel inspired about this, not giving up, being passionate about what you want to achieve, being compelled to get to your destination. What is the Why behind your goals, what will it cost if you don't achieve it, what will you gain when you do achieve it. Change your identity to your new definition of yourself. There is no such thing as an unrealistic goal, you just need perfect timing. Your emotions must fully embrace your vision, you have to be living your dream before it actualises. How you see your future is much more important than what has happened in your past so a lot of this comes down to your own perspective. If you change the way you look at things, the things you look at change. "It's not what you look at that matters, it's what you see" (Henry David Thoreau). Let your passion drive you forward to achieve your desires as "passion is the genesis of genius" (Galileo).

Visualisation is, in essence, a mental rehearsal, creating images in the mind of owning or pursuing what you desire. This process is repeated and practiced every day using your imagination, and getting your emotions involved to the point where you can feel and see yourself doing what you are visualising. The idea here is to visualise that you are already in possession of what it is that you desire, you must live and feel as though it is happening now, the sub-conscious mind cannot distinguish between real and imaginary and it will begin to work on aligning your vision with your reality (see chapter1).

We have to work, develop and grow in our knowledge within our vision, with clear intention, to create a full picture of what we desire. We must feel wealthy before wealth materialises, feel healthy before healing takes place, or feel loved before we enter into a relationship. This process has to be repeated diligently and consistently and then as Dr Dispenza states we can change our mind and body in preparation for this future event.

10 Fear not:

Be strong! Fear not; Fear is man's only adversary. You face defeat whenever you are fearful, Fear of lack! Fear of failure! Fear of loss! Fear of personality! Fear of criticism! Fear robs you of all power, for you have lost your contact with the Universal Power House. Fear is faith turned upside down, when you are fearful you begin to attract the thing you fear: you are magnetising it (Florence Shinn).

Do not be afraid to be yourself, stand by your convictions and be persistent in pursuing your dreams, do not let other people or other things or circumstances make you feel afraid or anxious because when you are living from a place of fear you have no power. Fear is the exact opposite of faith and the two cannot co-exist. We are instructed over 90 times in the Bible "Fear not", this is not a suggestion but rather an instruction or a command. "We are not given a spirit of fear, but of power, love and a sound mind". (2 Timothy 1:7)

Our physical body reacts to fear for reasons of self-preservation, we automatically move into fight or flight mode which brings a rush of adrenalin, and the widening of arteries to pump more blood to the necessary areas we need to engage for our survival. This process, in short bursts, is a healthy and natural bodily response to danger or emergency. When this bodily response becomes frequent and out of context, we may then refer to it as a stress response. If we are anxious about work because we don't get along well with the boss or with a colleague, we may feel frustrated or angry or bitter when we are around them. We create the same bodily responses and chemical reactions as if we were in danger and fighting to survive, but there is no emergency or pressing danger to fight against or run from therefore our body is in conflict. If you have created such a fear within your sub-conscious mind, then every time you refresh these negative thoughts even away from the offending situation they can be reproduced as fear in their own right. Dr Joe Dispenza states "if thoughts are the language of your brain and feelings are the language of your body, then every time you think about your problems past or present, you attach emotions to them and give away your power".

To experience a feeling, you must first entertain the thought that produced it, so try to take your thoughts captive and keep focus on the positive. Affirm in your mind, and out loud how you would like your life to be. "What you declare and decree with your mouth shall be established" (Job 22:28). Avoid worry, worry makes you focus on your problems instead of on God's promises, it is a pointless exercise, a bit like being in a rocking chair, it gives you something to do but gets you nowhere. Try not to see things as problems or obstacles but rather as a challenge, something new to conquer. "Some men see things as they are and say, why? I dream of things that never were and say why not?" (George Bernard Shaw).

Life is an opportunity, not a risk, so don't run from perceived danger, overcome it. Your time is better spent thinking about and focussing upon the solution rather than the problem, so go as far as you can go in faith, and then take one more step.

Whenever you visualise past trauma or hurt you are wiring new brain circuitry, if this past hurt created fear within your sub conscious, then you may be damaging your immune system. Every time you dwell on these negative thoughts, you are causing a chemical response to something that is now completely out of time and context but is producing fear in its own right, this will shut down your body's defence mechanisms. Some people live the majority of their lives in a state of constant stress either through work or life circumstance, this is not a position of creativity, inspiration, peace or happiness. Being in a constant state of stress puts your body into perpetual fight or flight mode and will ultimately cause disease if prolonged indefinitely.

The Bible has some sobering, and some comforting words to say on this subject, so I will close this short chapter with a selection of the many verses addressing this. "Do not be anxious about anything, but in every situation by prayer and petition, with thanksgiving, present your requests to God. And the peace of God which transcends all understanding, will guard your hearts and minds in Christ Jesus" (Philippians 4:6-7). "Therefore, I tell you, do not worry about your life, what you will eat or drink; or about your body, what you will wear. Is not life more than food, and the body more than clothes? Look at the birds of the air; they do not sow or reap or store away in barns, and yet your heavenly Father feeds them. Are you not much more valuable than they? Can any one of you by worrying add a single hour to your life? And why do you worry about clothes? See how the flowers of the field grow. They do not labour or spin. Yet I tell you that not even Solomon in all his splendour was dressed like one of these. If that is how God clothes the grass of the fields, which is here today and tomorrow is thrown into the fire, will He not much more cloth you – you of little faith? So, do not worry saying what shall we eat? Or what shall we drink? Or what shall we wear? For the pagans run after all these things, and your heavenly Father knows that you need them. But seek first His kingdom and His righteousness, and all these things will be given to you as well" (Mathew 6: 25 -33). "I sought the Lord, and he heard me, and delivered me from all my fears" (Psalm 34:4).

11 The secret place:

"Embrace the silence, enter the secret place, connect with your source. You are on Holy ground, don't enter lightly, intimate reverence with your God is mighty. Quiet contemplation He

rewards openly, His Divine nature constantly blessing me. Stillness is the quietening of the soul, shutting out everything, letting His wonder in, partake of Divine nature when He calls, don't go back off to sleep, these are secrets to keep. Tranquillity and time for you to learn, enter the healing flow, draw close to one who knows. His peacefulness is here, be still and know, thirst He will satisfy, hunger intensify" (P. Cawley – Secret place)

"But when you pray, go into your secret place, close the door and pray to your Father, who is unseen. Then your Father, who sees you in secret shall reward you openly" (Mathew 6:6)

The secret place is mentioned several times in the Bible and refers to going into your closet or quiet room to spend time with God in quiet contemplation and communion. I have a room at the back of my house overlooking the garden, which is my music room come office, it is the quietest room in the house due to the soundproofing work I did when we converted it. It is peaceful, still and tranquil in the early hours, and ideal for spiritual connection, creativity and reflection. When I go into this room each morning it feels kind of hallowed and set apart for higher purpose. It is a time of openness, gratitude and forgiveness from a humble and contrite heart. I have often been lost in the moment when time becomes transient, with no frame of reference, only later do I realise how much earth time has passed.

My early morning will then transition into a time devoted to reading scripture and prayer and will include expressing gratitude for all the many blessings I am thankful for. I will then ask for a blessing on my family and all my endeavours. I will usually end my time in my secret place by visualising my desired future and letting my imagination flow and involving my emotions in this process. I will then speak positive affirmations over my life and my family, my health and finances etc. (see chapter 14) Now in a calm and peaceful frame of mind and spiritually connected I will take a few minutes to reflect my thoughts, aspirations and feelings and plan my day in my journal. (See chapter 12)

This quiet time of spiritual awareness and enlightenment is sometimes referred to as the 'power hour'. Start the day with God, the divine intelligence, get into your secret place in perfect silence, be still and know!!, connect with your source, the source of all that is good, get beyond the analytical mind, get beyond yourself, meditate on your desires and your dreams and picture how it feels and smells, the peace it brings, the energy, the perfection of God. Away from all sensory stimuli and with eyes closed you can reduce beta brain waves of the analytical mind and increase alpha brain waves where we find peace, calm, stillness, inspiration and creativity and deeper thought.

Prayer:
I just want to add a few gems of wisdom here which will save you a lot of time and disappointment. Charles Capps in his book "Pray this Way" gives clear direction from the Bible on how to get your prayers answered. He cautions us about praying "if it be Your will", as this has opened the doors to fear and uncertainty too many times. God's will has been revealed clearly, over and over again in the Bible. Jesus tells us to pray the Lord's prayer in Mathew 6: 9-13 which clearly states "Your kingdom come Your will be done on earth as in Heaven". God's will in Heaven is for our good, for perfection, so if we are praying in accordance with the word of God, it will always be His will. Do not pray contrary to the word of God and expect results, do not pray the problem, if you pray from a position of defeat, then defeat is what you will compound. If, when you pray, you are saying, my health is getting worse, so please help me, you are in

effect having faith in the enemy, or in fear and not in God, you are walking by sight and not by faith, and so denying the word of God. Mark 11:24 states "Therefore I tell you, whatever you ask for in prayer, believe that you have received it, and it will be yours. And when you stand praying, if you hold anything against anyone, forgive them, so that your Father in heaven may forgive you your sins". We are also not supposed to pray to Jesus as this is unscriptural; Jesus said in John 16:23-24 "In that day you will no longer ask me anything. Very truly I tell you, my Father will give you whatever you ask in my name. Until now you have not asked for anything in my name. Ask and you will receive, and your joy will be complete". Prayer will bring God into your reality if your words are chosen carefully and spoken in the correct way according to scripture.

God has seen your future already and He will seat you with kings so run your race and shine. It is time to step up, shift gears and discipline yourself, you have been strategically positioned and there is a plan for your life. Stop looking back, the past is gone we are in the future with the architect of the ages, all things are possible for those who believe. Rise above religion, people need God, it is time to manifest as children of God to bring on the harvest. We are the manifested sons and daughters, this is the kingdom age and we are to call the things that are not as though they are, we were born for such a time as this, we are not here on earth at this time by accident. Put your faith firmly in God, keep your faith strong and follow diligently the calling you have received, you know exactly and unwaveringly what your calling is, don't let anyone stop or divert your journey.

Spending this quality time in the quiet early hours of the day will allow divine inspiration to flow through you and generate and grow your innate creativity and vision to fulfil your destiny. Spend much time with God, His word is immutable and it will come to pass, so stand on His promises. We are in the kingdom age and this will bring new demonstration and manifestation, don't be afraid of what people might say, because ultimately people want to hear the truth, they want reality not religion. This magical time of spiritual reflection is invaluable and allows you to partake of the divine nature, to connect with the Architect of the universe. The fear and reverence of God is the beginning of wisdom.

"As the heavens are higher than the earth, so are my ways higher than your ways and my thoughts

than your thoughts. As the rain and snow come down from heaven and do not return to it without watering the earth and making it bud and flourish, so that it yields seed for the sower and bread for the eater; so is my word that goes out from my mouth: It will not return to me empty but will accomplish what I desire and achieve the purpose for which I sent it" (Isaiah 55:9-11).

12 Journaling

"imagination is everything. It is the preview of life's coming attractions" Albert Einstein.

We are only limited by our own imagination. We must explore our thoughts and dreams and plan and write our future. *"The earth turns on its orbit for you. The oceans ebb and flow for you. The birds sing for you. The sun rises and sets for you. The stars come out for you. Every beautiful thing you see, every wonderous thing you experience, Is all there for you"* (Rhonda Byrne).

Why Journal

"History will be kind to me for I intend to write it" (Winston Churchill).

Research shows beyond any doubt that those who keep a journal are more prosperous than those who do not. There is evidence to show that regular journaling strengthens our immunity and our memory and helps us gain control of our emotions and mental health. Journaling reduces stress and helps us prioritise perceived problems, self-reflection helps us to identify negative thought and behaviour and clarify our thinking so we can get to know ourselves better. Journaling allows us to recognise our strengths and to build on them over time, to develop new and heightened perspective and bring a greater lust for life. Journaling helps us to organise our thoughts and to set and achieve our goals. Journaling is a great way to unleash your inspired creativity and let your imagination run wild. Thoughts become things and Journaling is a way of writing your day before it begins. "Never start a day until you have finished it in writing" (Jim Rhon).

Some ideas to get you started

Here are some ideas to help you on your way if this is your first time. Think about what motivates you; your plans to create a better life, what you have accomplished and what you want to accomplish next. Think of how you could improve your life by doing things differently (you will never make positive change by repeating what you always do). What are your ultimate desires and dreams, what is on your bucket list, where are you spiritually, what are you grateful for in your life, what are you pleased about and what makes you anxious? What do you want your life to look like in 1 year, 5 years or 10 years? What are the biggest lessons you have learned so far in life and how has that helped you, how would you advise a younger version of you, what gems of wisdom can you pass on to your children? Plan into your life some random acts of kindness to bless others less fortunate than you. What areas of your life could you improve on, in work, relationships etc, what are your best and worse character traits and how can you develop these areas. What are you gifted in, what would you do with your life if money was no object and you knew you couldn't fail.

"Logic will get you from A to B. Imagination will take you everywhere" (Albert Einstein).

Our thoughts and our words form our actions and create our future. Putting time aside daily to take our thoughts captive, to affirm and visualise who we are and where we want to be, and then to write in our journal the essence of all this is invaluable. "As a man thinks in his heart, so is he" (Proverbs 23: 7).

This process will literally rewrite our future and enable us to achieve our desired vision rather than accepting what life throws our way. Tapping into these principles and spiritual laws daily will turn our dreams into reality. "Happiness is when what you think, say, and do are in harmony" (Mahatma Gandhi).

The invisible or the unseen is where all creation comes from. Your thoughts are invisible, your feelings are invisible, your beliefs are invisible. To understand how all creation comes from the invisible, take a look at anything created by a human being and you will find out without exception that it began in the invisible, with a thought. Thoughts become things, thoughts are cause and our material world is the effect.

Everyone is 100% committed to keeping their habits, this is fact, the trouble with this is that most of us have many less than desirable habits. It takes 21 days of consistent, conscious reinforcement to establish or change a single habit according to behaviour modification experts, this is the time it takes for the brain to create the neuropathways necessary for change. A journal maintained daily with adequate detail is likely to be one of the best habits anyone can adopt. "Fill the paper with the breathings of your heart" (William Wordsworth).

The purpose of your journal then is not as a diary, but as a vision of the future. If you want a different tomorrow then you have to do something today to make it happen. Your journal is the place to record what your vision of the future looks like When we give time for quiet thought and contemplation and we focus on good and positive things we are in a growth-oriented mode which encourages prosperity and success. When we are journaling, we are writing from the heart and revealing our deepest thoughts and desires. "If your dreams don't scare you, they are too small" (Richard Branson).

When writing your journal, you are;
- Defining your plan – giving a detailed description of your goals and desires with long term and short term aims.
- Imaging the results – spending time visualising what you have written, how does it look, smell, feel, picture it done

and live in that moment until it becomes your reality.
- Command the outcome – spoken outcome, give positive affirmation about who you are and what you will achieve. "I am calm, I am loved, I am successful, I am prosperous, I am favoured".

Useful prompts to format your page
You may choose not to use any of these prompts, or, you may find some of them useful to add to the pages in your journal, that's up to you.

Morning:
I am grateful for ……….
Daily affirmations. "I am ……….
What would make today great ……….
How can I help someone today ……….

Evening:
How could I have made today even better ……….
Amazing things that happened today ……….
Best lesson I learned today ………
How did I help someone today ……….

The suggestions above are by no means exhaustive but may help you to get started and punctuate your page. These are useful exercises to help you to create, plan and achieve your true vision of yourself. When writing your journal keep focussed on what is important to you; health, relationships, money, time, reputation, skills, desires, faith, and personal growth. Write as if you're free falling, no limitations, no restrictions or boundaries.

So, happy journaling, be the best you can, seize the day and create your world. Have the faith to move mountains, believe in yourself, you were created in the image of God, so think big, chase your dreams with passion and live an abundant life.

13 Healthy body, healthy mind *'food for thought'*

"Its health that is real wealth and not pieces of gold and silver" (Mahatma Gandhi).

In a book dedicated to becoming the best person you can be it would be incomplete and irresponsible of me if didn't look at health, diet and exercise. I will not be going into too much detail on this subject in this book as this will need to be a book in its own right but I will give a good grounding on the basics of health and fitness that have helped me over the last 20 years or so.

Diet

"When diet is wrong, medicine is of no use, when diet is right, medicine is of no need". I have experimented over the years with many diets to test out the claims they make in terms of health benefits. I have tried the ketogenic diet, carnivore diet, high protein, food combination diet etc and I have never found one pure diet to fit the bill for me. I exercise daily and like to ensure that I get plenty of protein to promote and preserve muscle but with enough fibre and some carbohydrates to fend off hunger throughout the day. I keep carbs low as this prevents excess weight gain, heartburn and bloating, and I try to consume carbs earlier in the day so they burn off when metabolism is higher. I avoid highly processed carbs as these have little nutritional value, so white bread, white rice, pasta etc are rarely in my diet. White foods generally tend to be nutritionally void and usually contain large amounts of unwanted chemicals used in the processing cycle, like bleach and various anti caking products. Try to eat foods that are the colour they were intended to be before any experimentation took place. A good rule of thumb is, only eat food made by God, natural foods, grown or reared as nature intended, if its man- made, avoid it like the plague. Once the commercial food industry gets its chemistry set out, to either "enhance flavour" (MSG), or to extend shelf life we begin the downhill slide of slowly eroding our bodies with carcinogenic poisons. "Those who think they have no time for healthy eating, will, sooner or later, have to find time for illness" (Edward Stanley).

Eating a nutritious diet for health, fitness and wellbeing, has to be a lifestyle. It needs to be one of our good habits, if it is not, then follow the advice previously stated and create a new habit, it only takes 21 days to form the new neuro pathways necessary for change, so stick to it conscientiously. "Let food be thy medicine, and let medicine be thy food" (Hippocrates). Ironically modern-day physicians, who have taken the Hippocratic oath, often do the opposite in their practice, ignoring most of nature's medicine, and throwing pharmaceuticals at everything.

Thomas Edison made a very forward thinking and

intuitive statement a century ago when he said "The doctor of the future will no longer treat the human frame with drugs, but rather will cure and prevent disease with nutrition".

The Bible states that each of us may eat and drink, and find satisfaction in our toil- this is the gift from God (Ecclesiastes 3: 10) This would have been good general advice historically, when all food was home grown and rich in minerals, and all meat consumed was hand reared, but sadly, this is far from the case now for most of us. We now live in a totally different world in terms of the food at our disposal, and sometimes what is on offer from the supermarkets has been tampered with in one way or another either genetically modified with who knows what, or injected with antibiotics of some description. I think we need to pay more attention to another Bible verse "My people perish for lack of knowledge" (Hosea 4:6), it is vital in this day to read the packaging your food comes in and to buy fresh wherever possible. Do not buy foods which contain the following chemicals as they all have harmful effects on your health; Monosodium Glutamate (MSG), artificial food colouring, Sodium Nitrite/ all Nitrates and Nitrites, Guar gum, High Fructose Corn syrup, artificial sweeteners unless plant based (Stevia),

Sodium Benzoate, Trans fats, Xanthan gum, artificial flavouring, yeast extract. These are just some of the usual suspects which have been linked to many adverse side effects, try also to keep all processed food to a minimum and go fresh. "Life expectancy would grow by leaps and bounds if green vegetables smelled as good as bacon" (Doug Larson).

If fluctuating weight is a problem for you then you will need to focus on foods that increase your metabolism. Here is just a general basic guide of what you should include in your diet, and things to avoid or keep in careful moderation.

Protein - eat protein rich foods like meat, fish, eggs, dairy and nuts. These foods require your body to use more energy to digest them (thermic effect) hence more calories burned, if you are in a regular exercise regime (which you should be) these foods will also help to maintain muscle mass. These foods are also rich in **Iron, Zinc & Selenium,** so play a part in controlling your thyroid gland which regulates your metabolism. There are many spices which also boost metabolism and these include ginger, cayenne pepper, turmeric and others which have many other health benefits.

Leafy greens – leafy green vegetables are an important part of a healthy diet, they are packed with vitamins, minerals and fibre, but are very low in calories. A diet rich in leafy greens has many health benefits including the reduction of heart disease, high blood pressure and obesity and also has a positive effect on mental agility. Foods to include in your diet will include kale, collard greens, spinach, cabbage, watercress and lettuce to name a few and these can be found all year round to incorporate into your weekly diet.

Refined sugars – Refined sugars in the form of sucrose and high fructose corn syrup are found in the majority of processed food from ketchup to coffee whitener and excessive and long-term use of any products containing these elements can lead to chronic illnesses including heart problems, type 2 diabetes and stroke. Get into the habit of reading food packaging, you can be fooled into thinking that some breakfast cereal and yogurt is a healthy option, but these can often be loaded with refined sugars too so be careful. If chocolate is one of your cravings then try to switch to dark chocolate, 80% and above is a much healthier option. When reading your food labels be aware that the food industry has over 50 different names for refined sugar so do your homework.

Fats – incorporate more healthy fats into your diet like avocado and olive oil, coconut oil, olives, nuts, fatty fish, soybean products. These fats, are good for your heart, your cholesterol and your overall health, this is why the Mediterranean diet is so good for health and longevity.

Water – The human body is made up of about 70% water, so there must be a hint in there that water is a pretty important to human beings. We must all consume a certain amount of water to survive, this can vary dependent on environment and stature but generally men need about 3 litres and women 2.2 litres. The recommended daily water consumption for men in a temperate climate is nearer 4 litres per day and 3 litres for women increasing this further when engaged in exercise. Where possible always drink filtered water. Drinking filtered water is better for overall health, the removal of Chlorine and Fluoride from your drinking water can reduce the risk of rectal, colon and bowel cancer. In some areas there may also be traces of Arsenic which is a powerful carcinogenic linked to many cancers and Aluminium traces in water supplies has been linked to Alzheimer's disease, skin disorders, liver problems and hyperactivity in children. A large glass of filtered water first thing in the morning has many health benefits, it flushes out toxins, increases energy, boosts metabolism, helps weight loss, improves skin condition and strengthens the immune system. So, drink filtered water and plenty of it.

Intermittent fasting - Having spoken much about healthy diets, there is also many health benefits to be had from intermittent fasting. I have had periods of time when I have done this daily, but now tend to keep it to a couple of times per week, because for me, it caused unwanted weight loss. My intermittent fast would typically be to have a good meal around 6 pm and then not eat again until 11 am or later the following day, so a fast of over 16 hours. During this time, I will drink a lot of water and will have other drinks as well. Here are some of the benefits of intermittent fasting. Your body, during a fast goes into cellular repair mode changing hormones to make stored body fat more accessible. Blood insulin levels drop significantly which facilitates fat burning, the body goes into a cleansing process, eliminating waste from cells. Genetic change occurs relating to longevity and immunity. Short-term fasting produces higher growth hormone levels and noradrenaline which increase the breakdown of fat to use for energy, your metabolic rate significantly increases. Intermittent fasting can significantly reduce the risk of type 2 diabetes and reduce inflammation generally in the body. Intermittent fasting has been proven to reduce the risk of serious diseases like cancers and Alzheimer's and improve general brain health. In short, regular intermittent fasting has a very positive effect on health and longevity, why not give it a try and maybe incorporate it into your health and fitness programme.

Supplements – Enhancing our healthy diet with vitamin and mineral supplementation is a practice that I adhere to every day. Back in the days when food was home grown and reared, people knew what they were getting and fresh produce from mineral rich soils would have provided the majority of nutrients essential for a healthy life. Sadly, most of us do not live, in situations and environments where this kind of lifestyle is possible, and, given the lack of nutrients and added poisons in typical supermarket food that I have discussed, it is vital to ensure we are giving ourselves the best chances of health by supplementation. There are 13 essential vitamins and 7 major minerals with many more subsidiary minerals required by the body for optimum daily functioning and we simply will not get these in a typical western diet. I tend to supplement with a reputable multi-vitamin & mineral supplement as a bed rock and then I boost my health with the following additions. 1000mg vitamin C, 125mcg or vitamin D, 2500mg Turmeric, 200mcg Selenium, 225mcg Sea Kelp, 40mg Zinc and 370mg Magnesium. A bumper dose of vitamin C and D are essential during current pandemic times to keep an optimum immune system. I take a daily dose of apple cider vinegar also but I will discuss this in the next section.

The last thing on food and drink, is keep your alcohol consumption in moderation, you don't need me to give any explanation here as to why, and I don't wish to insult anyone's intelligence. Just do it!

Exercise (Here we go !!)
"Physical fitness is not only one of the most important keys to a healthy body, it is the basis of dynamic and creative intellectual activity". John F Kennedy

Regular physical activity not only improves muscle strength and endurance, it also delivers oxygen and nutrients to your tissues and helps your cardiovascular system to function more efficiently, if this doesn't impress you, it also boosts your mood and your sex life and increases longevity. With all exercise, consistency is the key, occasional bursts of exercise maybe fun but will be of little consequence health wise. Regular exercise, just like a healthy diet reaps dividends helping to prevent many chronic illnesses, mental health problems and arthritis. Exercise boosts energy due to increased circulation and promotes better sleep. Regular exercise has been proven to increase sexual arousal in women and men who exercise regularly are less likely to suffer with erectile dysfunction. Try to aim for 60 minutes of aerobic exercise per week and strength training exercise 3 times per week or more.

Supplementation can enhance your results when you follow a heathy diet and take regular exercise. I tend to take creatine monohydrate and a testosterone booster before my daily exercise, but I am in my 50's and these may not be necessary for you. Don't be naïve though about this, it is a fact that men's testosterone levels begin to fall in their late 20's and then continue for the rest of your life. Testosterone rich foods and regular resistance workouts with weights will significantly help maintain good levels. I then follow, after exercise with a Whey protein drink and mix in a raw egg and a slug of cider vinegar, this helps repair and maintain muscle mass. Apple cider vinegar boosts metabolism, increases energy, helps digestion, breaks down bad bacteria and feeds good bacteria, and also helps prevent blood sugar spikes, Braggs is one of the better brands. I take Zinc and Magnesium Aspartate (ZMA) an hour before bed time, this combination in high dose also maintains testosterone levels and aids restful sleep.

I exercise early morning and do a full body workout. I do body-weight leg raises, squats and step ups (15 minutes), Standard press ups and inverted press ups, 300-400 (20 minutes), Abdominal exercises on a mat, leg raises, bikes, crunches etc, (15 minutes), Arm exercises, body weight dips, resistance band curls single arm alternating to failure (15 minutes). I do this most mornings and this allows me to get breathless with the leg exercises, and to muscle failure with the resistance training. I also have a small gym at home so I like to use this a couple of times per week, on those days I will substitute the previously mentioned exercises with weights, bench presses, kettlebells and dumbbell reps and then I will have a 10 minute fast run on the treadmill. This is just an example, do what suits you and fits in with your life. In the nicer weather I like to also go cycling, walking and running. I always try to push for one more rep, or to run that bit further or faster, set some challenges to beat your personal best, keep it fun and keep it going.

14 Power Hour & Mighty Morning

I have tried to condense a lot of information and research into a more digestible, understandable and user-friendly guide to techniques and disciplines, which if followed consistently, will bear much fruit, physically, mentally, emotionally and spiritually. I would like to draw this book to an end by documenting a typical morning living life this way, putting into practice the ideas and concepts described and how I feel ready to take on the world by 6.30 am.

A disciplined start to the day is where we begin, my alarm is set but I rarely need it as my body clock wakes me anytime from 4 am, don't go back off to sleep, it is always worth the sacrifice. Washed, teeth brushed and downstairs in 5 minutes, I have a long drink of cold water and then I go into my music room, the lighting is calm and relaxing and the peacefulness of the room in the early hours often feels magical, spiritual, with an air of expectancy and anticipation.

I often pick up one of my guitars and play very quietly for a while, usually a worshipful song will come to mind and I may get lost in it for a while. I will usually then naturally transition into prayer. The things I say will begin with what I am grateful for, a new day, breath in my lungs, sight in my eyes, health, fitness, my family, home, material possessions. I will be humble before a mighty God knowing that He always hears me. I will pray in detail about personal things and make my requests to God asking for His blessing on my life, my family and all my endeavours. I will pray for the country and for wisdom for its leaders, for world affairs and for peace and prosperity in Israel. I will then pray for wisdom, knowledge, discernment and understanding, for divine inspiration and creativity to fulfil my destiny. I will often at this point take Communion and remember the death of Jesus and the victory through the resurrection which made a way.

I usually ask for a blessing on my business endeavours and I spend a while visualising how my life will be as I make steps towards fulfilling my destiny. I get into the mindset of "picturing it done", I visualise what it will look like, how it will feel, smell and sound, I live the life before the event and enjoy the excitement and satisfaction of this with humility and gratitude. (See chapter 9).

I will then begin to affirm who I am and what I expect from my day and what is available to me. (see chapter 8). Positive affirmations are using the power of words (see chapter 3), speak your day into being before it begins. For example;

- Everything works together for good for me today
- My inspiration comes from God "infinite intelligence"
- Divine substance blesses me with abundance
- I recognise and accept the divine plan for my life which includes health, wealth, happiness and perfect self-expression.
- I am created in the image of God, no illness can come upon me, I affirm divine health.
- With me is the wisdom of ages which shows me how to expand my life, prosper and help others.

- My mind is renewed by the word of God and therefore I forbid any thoughts of failure, lack, defeat or limitation in my mind. ………………………..

I then will spend time studying scripture and other writings, gleaning nuggets of wisdom and revelation which serve to get my day into perspective. I will then take a few minutes to write in my journal and write my day start to finish before it begins. (see chapter 12)

I will now have a cold drink of water and take my pre workout supplements and move into my front room for my workout. This is usually around 5.30 am so too early to use my upstairs gym as it would be too noisy. I am a You tube addict, so, I always have a lot of things lined up on my smart tv of an inspirational or spiritual nature, so I can listen and learn and enrich my knowledge whilst working out. I follow the workout outlined in the previous chapter. I will then have a large reinforced protein shake and take my daily supplements.

Usually by 6 to 6.30 am, I am refreshed, connected, alert and ready to seize the day, the one I have planned. The 'power hour' I have described usually does last about an hour then another 45 minutes to an hour of exercise and continued learning and inspiration. Being geared up inspirationally, spiritually, mentally and physically by the time a lot of people are just waking up is a great use of my time, puts me ahead of my game and whilst I then enjoy a coffee as the world awakes, I can reflect on my morning and look forward to it unfolding.

I hope you can use some of what I have written to develop and enhance your own mighty mornings, and feel the benefits gained, by being completely in control of your thoughts, words, vision and physical health and to enable you to hit the ground running every day.

In this day and age when everyone has a least one device able to connect to the internet, ignorance is a choice. Learn something new each day, this fires up neurones and creates neuro pathways enhancing mental capacity (neuro-plasticity). Life is an ongoing education and there is so much information available to us for free, we have no excuses anymore. Set time aside to read inspiring books, or, if you're not much of a reader, get audio books or use You tube or any of the other information platforms, listen to seminars, talks and testimonials of people you admire and who you would aspire to emulate.

Throughout your day remember that you started well, so keep going and finish well also. Prepare healthy foods and snack to sustain you until you get home for dinner. If you have a sedentary job, try to make a regular point of getting up and walking around for a while. A quick walk at lunch time can revitalise, and remember to keep on top of your water intake.

Perform your tasks to the best of your ability and go the extra mile. Look for ways to help others who may be struggling, remember how it felt when you were at their level, they will always remember your kind acts. If you drive to work, leave in good time so that you are calm and not rushed, try letting others out of their junctions, they are also trying to get to work, a splash of human kindness will help them and also bless you. Remind yourself throughout the day what you are grateful for and don't take anything for granted.

Know and reflect upon what you want outside of the 9-5 job and follow your vision, there is ready provision, strive to fulfil your destiny. If you could make a living doing what you love, this is probably your gifting, pursue it with passion and one day it will become your living as well as your dream. Never forget "Thoughts become things"

Invest time in education, never stop learning, reading and developing in knowledge, skills and character. Optimise good relationships and invest in them, and avoid bad ones as they will only serve to rag you down. Develop a zero tolerance to negativity, and this includes your own negative thoughts, dismiss them as they land in your mind, replace them with positive and uplifting, solution focussed thoughts which are of help to you and those around you.

Find time for leisure time and hobbies, diarise them, and give them the importance they should have so that your evenings and weekends have fun, substance and excitement and are not just a quick pause between Friday evening and Monday morning. When bedtime comes around, which it does all too quickly, wind down properly. I'm probably preaching to the converted, but avoid too much screen time leading up to bed, unless you have an adapted kindle reader, be old school and read something made of paper, like books, remember them? something wholesome before sleep, then you will be naturally rested and your dreams will be flavoured with the story you were reading. If you have trouble sleeping, as I intermittently do, then try not to eat or drink too much an hour before bed, ensure your room is completely dark when it's time to sleep and keep to a good sleep routine in terms of time. Natural sleep aids like 5HPT, melatonin, camomile can be useful, and for guys, remember to take ZMA an hour before bed for better quality sleep and an overnight testosterone boost, and we all need it from 30 years onwards.

Conclusion

Be as true at being yourself as you can, when you were a child you didn't disguise your differences, your likes and dislikes, what you were good at, instead you showed off these skills unabashedly. The truth is we are all unique and have our individual giftings and talents, no one can be you as well as you can, so instead of hiding your essence and your passion, celebrate it, and capitalise on the skills you have. Stop trying to meet the approval of others and what they think you ought to be doing with your life at the expense of being yourself. Often, the perception others have of you is way left of field anyway, so be true to yourself, and don't hide behind a false ego you have developed for self-preservation purposes, the ego has often been described as "edging God out" and often takes with it your true spirit and humility. So be truly humble, humility is not thinking less about yourself, but rather thinking about yourself less as someone once quoted. So "humble yourself in the eyes of the Lord, and He will lift you up"

Do not doubt your abilities in anyway, you are special. Let your life be your message as Mahatma Gandhi once said. We are all spirit, we have a soul and we live in a body and we are connected to a higher intelligence, we all have a mission to fulfil and a message to bring to enhance the life experience of others. Listen to your inner voice, the still small voice within you, just like you did as a child.

Taking action now is of the utmost importance, do not procrastinate from being and achieving everything you want to be. Don't waste time pursuing other jobs and positions of interest just to build up a good and interesting resume in the hope of eventually getting to where you want to be, this is like saving sex for old age as Warren

Buffett one said. Activate your passion now, get involved in making your dreams a reality. "Start before you're ready, don't prepare, begin" (Mel Robbins). "Fight the good fight, finish the race and keep the faith" (2 Timothy 4:7).

The rest of your day starts with one decision to seize the day or hit the snooze button, to embrace a planned day from your perspective, or to fall into Monday morning sideways. Mel Robins, American TV host suggests a 5 second rule to acting on things you might ordinarily put off. So, when the alarm goes off and you don't want to get up, count back 5 4 3 2 1 then just do it before your mind tries to persuade you otherwise. You can't always control how you will feel, but you can take the emotion out and control how you will act, start before you're ready, don't prepare, begin. You have been assigned this mountain so that you can show others how it can be removed. The odds of you being born with your DNA and your life circumstances has been scientifically proven to be one in 400 trillion, you are very unique, very special with life changing ideas. (Mel Robins).

The human body is made of around 7 octillion atoms, with 70-100 trillion cells. Your heart beats

100,000 times per day and pumps 400 litres of blood per hour, 8 litres per minute, 100,000 times per day through 100,000 km of blood vessels. We make 10 million cells per second, because we lose 10 million cells per second. Each cell goes through the order of 100, 000 chemical reactions per second. Our stomach acid can dissolve metal, our skin sheds and repairs every 2-4 weeks. There are a trillion nerves powering your memory, your eyes can distinguish up to a million different colours. Your lungs inhale over 2 million litres of air daily. Your small intestine is 20-23 feet in length. Nerve impulses travel to the brain at speeds up to 250 miles per hour. Your bones are 4 times stronger than concrete. Your nose can distinguish 10,000 different smells, and you tongue has a similar number of taste buds. We are amazing products of creation with brain function outstripping even the most advanced and cutting-edge computer technology.

Our body does all this without us paying any attention to it, many people completely disregard the presence of the higher intelligence that gives us life, let alone spend time interacting with or having a relationship with this intelligence known to believers as God.

Take the time every morning to get in touch with yourself and your source, this is the best use of your time to begin each day, it makes you, into the real you, connected and at peace with God, and with your surroundings. Become the creative and inspired person you are meant to be, truly grateful for all your blessings and excited for the day that you have planned to unfold.

Your thoughts, become your words, which in turn influence your actions and lifestyle. Thoughts become things, and how you harness them will determine your level of success, your health, and your happiness, your spiritual connectedness, temperament and ultimate longevity. It is crucial that we get this right if we wish to achieve true freedom, fulfil our destiny and become the best versions of ourselves.

Rewrite your current story, go back to the original book, where nothing is impossible, with childlike faith, and live it like you cannot fail. Your history doesn't have to be your future, break the generational chains and curses and be a trailblazer, cut out a new way for the future generations to follow.

Become the real you; this is your life, don't be a passenger.

About the Author

Phil Cawley was born in South Yorkshire where he lived until age 10 then the family moved to the North East of England. Phil lived in Sunderland until his late 20's, after graduating at Sunderland University with an Honours Degree, majoring in Psychology. Phil has completed many further courses and studies at Degree and Masters level, mostly in Management.

Phil is a Christian family man who currently lives in Buckinghamshire in the South East of England. He has worked for the local authority as a frontline worker, then as a manager for most of his working life. Working in a variety of settings helping and enabling children, young people and their families, in challenging circumstances, to make positive change and improve their life chances. Despite the immense rewards of this vocation, Phil became disillusioned with the bureaucratic facade within the department so took his leave to pursue long awaited creative projects which have always been a burning passion.

Phil currently spends most of his time working on writing projects and also writing and producing music.

Phil enjoys spending time with family, especially his little Grand Daughter, and has many hobbies including song writing, playing guitar, working out, fishing and cycling.

Other books by this Author

The Blood & The Glory

The blood of Jesus, the most precious of all, was freely shed for the salvation of mankind and avails for all who believe. The blood of Jesus used to be preached as a priority, in earlier days of the Church. The 'old timers' knew the power that could be invoked, and the healing and miracles that followed. Many of the songs sung in churches would include the power in the blood. This subject matter, the true essence of Christianity, seems sadly lacking in many church's today, with preference given instead to motivational feel-good messages.

This book, however, will focus entirely on the quintessential Christian message of the blood of Jesus Christ, with no provisos or excuses made. This book will no doubt offend many people, get over it. I intend to present an

Iterated message of The Way, The truth and The Life, the embodiment of Jesus Christ, the crucial message of the Blood and the Glory.

Be Inspired: Volume 1

Wise words to encourage, move and motivate, to breathe life, spark ideas and impassion your day.

Wise and wonderful words from positive thinkers is a tonic to the heart and soul and gears us up, mentally and physically, for what is ahead. When we reframe our thinking, we can look at our situations differently, and when we change the way we look at things, the things we look at change. A refreshing injection of positive thought can revitalise our thought processes and make us resonate with the joys of life and with new focus on getting the best for our lives and that of others.

This inspirational collection of quotes, some famous, some not so well known, will be a great companion for many situations. Your morning devotions, coffee breaks at work, a little book to pack in your holiday bag or your daily commute to and from work. "A word of encouragement

echoes
of the heart